Tackling Cyberbullying and Related Problems

This book looks at innovative tools developed by Japanese and Korean researchers and practitioners to tackle cyberbullying and internet-related problems (addiction, cybercrimes, etc.). The contributors have created preventative and intervention measures for children using games, apps, manga and anime videos, which are more accessible for children than textbooks or classroom-based lessons. The contributors cover their experiences of developing these new approaches with children, parents and teachers as well as giving insights and evidence into how these innovative techniques and methods work. By sharing their expertise, the authors hope to contribute to further improvements of games, apps, manga and anime and to improve the safety of children online.

Yuichi Toda is Professor of Education at Osaka Kyoiku University, Japan.

Insoo Oh is Professor in the College of Education at Ewha Womans University, South Korea.

Tackling Cyberbullying and Related Problems

Innovative Usage of Games, Apps and Manga

Edited by Yuichi Toda and Insoo Oh

Routledge
Taylor & Francis Group
LONDON AND NEW YORK

First published 2021
by Routledge
2 Park Square, Milton Park, Abingdon, Oxon OX14 4RN

and by Routledge
52 Vanderbilt Avenue, New York, NY 10017

Routledge is an imprint of the Taylor & Francis Group, an informa business

British Library Cataloguing-in-Publication Data
A catalogue record for this book is available from the British Library

Library of Congress Cataloging-in-Publication Data
Names: Toda, Yuichi, editor. | Oh, Insoo, editor.
Title: Tackling cyberbullying and related problems: Innovative
usage of games, apps and manga / edited by Yuichi Toda, Insoo Oh.
Description: New York: Routledge, 2020. |
Includes bibliographical references and index.
Identifiers: LCCN 2020026024 (print) |
LCCN 2020026025 (ebook) | ISBN 9780367202422 (hardback) |
ISBN 9780429260384 (ebook)
Subjects: LCSH: Cyberbullying. | Cyberbullying–Prevention. |
Internet addiction. | Internet–Psychological aspects.
Classification: LCC HV6773.15.C92 T33 2020 (print) |
LCC HV6773.15.C92 (ebook) | DDC 302.34/3–dc23
LC record available at https://lccn.loc.gov/2020026024
LC ebook record available at https://lccn.loc.gov/2020026025

ISBN: 978-0-367-20242-2 (hbk)
ISBN: 978-0-429-26038-4 (ebk)

Typeset in Times New Roman
by Newgen Publishing UK

Contents

Figures

Tables

Contributors

Editors

Yuichi Toda: Professor, Faculty of Education, Osaka Kyoiku University, Osaka, Japan

Insoo Oh: Professor, the College of Education, Ewha Womans University, Seoul, South Korea

Chapter Contributors

Brent Allison: Professor, the College of Education, University of North Georgia, Georgia, US

Stephanie S. Fredrick: Assistant Professor and Associate Director of the Dr. Jean M. Alberti Center for the Prevention of Bullying Abuse and School Violence, the University at Buffalo, State University of New York, Buffalo, NY, US

Ram Herkanaidu: PhD Security Researcher, the Centre for Security, Communications and Network Research, University of Plymouth, Plymouth, UK

Akihiko Ieshima: Associate Professor, Career Center, Osaka University, Osaka, Japan

Kazuhiko Ishihara: Professor, Faculty of Education, Gifu Shotoku Gakuen University, Gifu, Japan

Tomoyuki Kanetsuna: Associate Professor, Professional Graduate School for Teacher Education, Kagawa University, Kagawa, Japan

Samuel Y. Kim: Assistant Professor and Director of the Specialist in School Psychology Program in the Department of Psychology and Philosophy, Texas Woman's University, Denton, TX, US

Natalia Kucirkova: Professor of Early Childhood and Development, Norwegian Centre for Learning Environment, University of Stavanger, Stavanger, Norway

Ruthaychonnee Sittichai: Associate Professor of Behavioural Sciences, Faculty of Humanities and Social Sciences, Kids and Youth Development Research Unit, Prince of Songkla University, Pattani, Thailand

Yi-Shan Tsai: Research Associate, School of Informatics, University of Edinburgh, Edinburgh, UK

Toshiro Tsuruta: Assistant Professor, Faculty of Health Sciences, Odawara campus, International University of Health and Welfare, Kanagawa, Japan

Tomoya Yamamoto: Teacher, Junior & Senior High School at Komaba, University of Tsukuba, Tokyo, Japan

Hyung Sup Yoon: Professor and Dean of Game School, Jilin Animation Institute, Jilin, China

Foreword

Bullying (*ijime* in Japanese, *wang-ta* in Korean and *qifu* in Chinese) has been recognized as a universal problem which endangers children's physical and mental health, even causing irreparable and devastating outcomes for both victims and bullies, such as suicide and committing crime. In the Internet era, bullying has been reinforced by the increasing use of information and communication technologies. Along with all the merits cyberspace has brought to us, characteristics of cyber communication such as anonymity and rapid circulation make cyberbullying easier to perpetrate and more covert, leading to new concerns for the public and new research topics for the international academic community.

Systematic study on school bullying originated in Scandinavia in the 1980s, and most of the research over the last 40 years has been in Western countries. It has been reflected in the *Handbook of Bullying in Schools: An International Perspective* (Jimerson, Swearer and Espelage, 2010) and relevant international journal publications. Despite the general lack of research on bullying in Eastern countries, study on *ijime* in Japan and *wang-ta* in Korea got started fairly early in the 1980s and 1990s and both have developed their own traditions. This book brings together the research and prevention/intervention efforts of colleagues in the area of school bullying in these two countries, providing valuable information about the characteristics of school bullying and important implications for school bullying prevention/intervention in Eastern countries. In particular, this book explores the possibility of using games, apps and manga in tackling bullying, and provides the successful examples of "Angry Daddy" and "117 Chat".

Professor Yuichi Toda and I met at the ISSBD Biennial Meeting in Beijing in 2000. In 2005, he invited me to visit Osaka Kyoiku University and I talked about my research on bullying in China. In October 2019, I organized the *International Conference on Prevention and Interventions of School Bullying* in Jinan, China, at which Yuichi delivered his keynote speech. For two decades, we have kept in touch and have been more close friends than just colleagues. I take this opportunity to congratulate professors Yuichi Toda and Insoo Oh for the publication of this book and look forward to the important contributions it will make to school bullying research and intervention at regional and international levels.

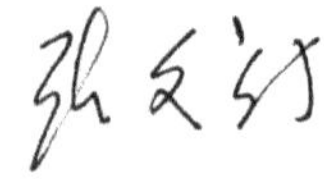

Wenxin Zhang, Ph.D.
Professor at Shandong Normal University
Director of School Bullying Research Center at
Shandong Normal University
Chairperson of School Bullying and Violence Specialized
Committee of Chinese Psychological Society
May 2020
Jinan, China

Preface

This book emerges from the close collaboration of researchers from South Korea and Japan. These two countries are experiencing political conflicts related to historical matters. However, in terms of cultural and economic aspects, the two countries share many similarities and are mutually influencing. The editors first collaborated in a trinational symposium in 2015 in Nagoya, Japan, at the JPA (The Japanese Psychological Association) 79th Annual meeting, at which we were also joined by Prof. Zhang Wenxin, who has written the Foreword for this book. Researchers from China, South Korea and Japan came together to discuss various aspects of bullying. Soon after the JPA meeting, the editors held a symposium together at the 32nd International Congress of Psychology in 2016, after which we discussed the potential publication of our collaborative works with an editor from Routledge. Over the following four years we collaborated with colleagues in South Korea and Japan, and internationally, to plan and write this book.

We hope that our introduction of apps, manga and related innovative approaches to preventing bullying will be useful to readers in tackling cyberbullying and other related problems. As these problems are shared beyond national borders, it will be effective for researchers and practitioners to collaborate internationally in order to protect children regardless of their nationality or background. Apps from South Korea and manga from Japan are both effective in preventing bullying and introducing them together in this book may lead to new developments drawing on elements from both. The differences in certain aspects of cyberbullying due to the different cultural contexts will also be informative. Our models to capture the phenomenon and countermeasures should serve as an opportunity to promote more fruitful research and effective practices. As the problems are becoming much more complicated, we must expand our collaboration not just beyond international borders but also beyond disciplinary borders. In the future, our students will continue and expand this collaboration.

Finally, we express our gratitude to Routledge and our academic colleagues who have supported us in editing this book, and hope our students, colleagues, friends and family are safe and healthy during the Covid-19 pandemic.

Y. Toda and I. Oh

1 Traditional/cyberbullying and Internet-mediated problems in South Korea and Japan

Yuichi Toda and Insoo Oh

Nowadays, children are communicating in both cyberspace and face-to-face situations. Communicating online enables children to be reachable to a wider range of people. However, there are various risks alongside the benefits, with some vulnerable children suffering and some children causing trouble and even committing crimes. In order to avoid traditional bullying, cyberbullying, and Internet-mediated problems, preventive approaches have been introduced in both class lessons and PC games (Sainio et al., 2019; Salmivalli and Poskiparta, 2012). Although it is still early in the development of such efforts, we should focus on these new tactics and clarify the possible effects as well as the underlying obstacles to overcome. In this chapter, we will depict some of the similarities and differences of bullying in South Korea and Japan. This will provide a helpful background from which to better understand the prevention programs introduced in later chapters.

Short history of incidents of traditional/cyberbullying and Internet-mediated problems

In this section we will provide a short history of bullying, cyberbullying, and the Internet-mediated problems in both South Korea and Japan. We will also mention the results of some government surveys and discuss how the media focus has changed to show people's views on such problems in both countries.

Short history of bullying in South Korea

Here, we will summarise the history and definition of bullying and school violence. We will then discuss recent trends in bullying in Korea before turning to cyberbullying and its related problems. In South Korea, the most commonly used term associated with bullying is *wang-ta*. The term was coined in the mid-1990s when school violence sparked social concerns. The prefix "wang" means very severe and emphasises the following words: the word "ta" is an abbreviated term meaning "rejection". Consequently, *wang-ta* has established itself as Korea's unique term for bullying (Koo, Kwak, and Smith, 2008).

Currently, the two terms, bullying and school violence, are used interchangeably in Korea (Lee, 2014). The term "school violence" is used more frequently than the term "bullying", because violent behaviours between peers must be dealt with by a specific law on school violence. As such, bullying in Korea is strictly controlled on the basis of the Act on Prevention and Countermeasures of School Violence. The law defines school violence as follows:

> School violence is the act involving physical, mental, or property damage caused by injury, assault, imprisonment, intimidation, pillage, and inducement, defamation, blackmail, coercion and coercion of errands and sexual violence, bullying, cyber-bullying, and obscene or violent information using information and communication networks.

As explained above, school violence described by law can be categorised into eight types (Ministry of Education, 2014a):

- Physical violence: the act of beating or pushing the other person to inflict pain on victims.
- Verbal violence: the use abusive language, intimidating or defaming the other person.
- Extortion of valuables: the act of forcibly taking money or valuable items or asking for them and then not returning them.
- Compulsory demand: the act of forcing victims to do homework, to run errands, or to share smartphone data.
- Rejection: the act of deliberately ostracising, ignoring the victim, or spreading false rumours.
- Sexual violence: the act of making victims feel sexual shame, or making physical or verbal sexual remarks and actions.
- Cyberbullying: the act of swearing at or spreading false information or threatening others through Internet bulletin boards, chats, SNS (Social Networking Service), and so on.
- Stalking: the act of following up and harassing the victim despite the victim's opposition.

There are several points to note in this law. The first is that school violence is limited to violence against "students". Therefore, the law cannot be applied to cases of violence against teachers. Violence against teachers has recently been increasing, so this type of violence is drawing attention. Second, violence outside school can be dealt with by the law because the law provides the scope of violence that occurs "inside as well as outside of school". Finally, the law was first enacted in 2004 and then cyberbullying was added when it was revised in 2012. Other kinds of violence are now showing a tendency of decreasing, but, in contrast, cyberbullying is increasing.

The trend of the rates of school violence in South Korea is shown in Figure 1.1. The data comes from the annual survey conducted by the Youth

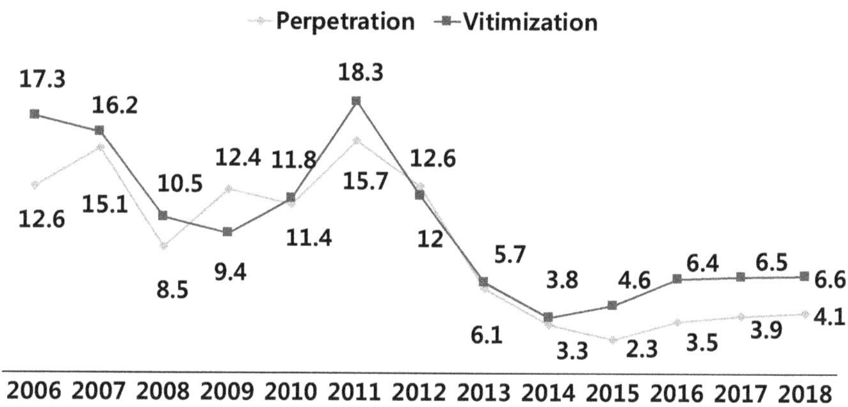

Figure 1.1 Trend of school violence 2006 through 2017 (YVPF).
Source: YVPF (2019). 2018 National School Violence Survey.

Violence Prevention Foundation (in short, "YVPF survey" in this chapter) since 2006. The figure shows that school violence has mostly been decreasing since 2012. That decline is also confirmed by the Ministry of Education's survey (in short, "MoE survey"). However, compared with the YVPF survey, the MoE survey shows relatively low rates of school violence. The reason for such a difference may partly be due to the difference of reference period of each survey. In general, longer reference periods (e.g., one semester to one year) tend to result in greater amounts of school violence being recorded. In addition, it may be due to differences in the number of survey questions. The more questions that are asked to identify school violence in questionnaires, the higher the recorded rate of school violence is (Song and Oh, 2015).

However, one of the similarities between those two surveys is that both suggest that school violence has been decreasing since 2012. Some may suggest that this is an effect of the Comprehensive School Violence Eradication Plan announced and implemented in 2012. Another notable commonality is that school violence, which has declined since 2012, has shown a slight increase again recently.

Figure 1.1 shows that school violence has decreased since 2012, but in contrast, cyberbullying is increasing (Ministry of Education, 2014b). Also, the MoE survey showed that cyberbullying increased steadily over the three-year period from 2015 to 2017. Another survey by Song and Oh (2015) also found that cyberbullying has increased, though traditional violence has decreased. Table 1.1 shows the rates of cyberbullying in comparison to other types of school violence (Ministry of Education, 2019). Given the total number of violence as 100%, cyberbullying is about 10.8% of the total; and it was more common among middle (15.0%) and high school (14.6%) students than elementary school (9.2%) children.

Table 1.1 The ratios by subtypes of school violence (Ministry of Education)

	Verbal Violence	*Group Rejection*	*Stalking*	*Physical Violence*	**Cyberbullying**	*Valuables Extortion*	*Sexual Violence*	*Compulsory Demand*
All	34.7	17.2	11.8	10.0	**10.8**	6.4	5.2	3.9
Elementary	34.5	16.2	13.4	10.6	**9.2**	6.6	5.3	4.2
Middle	35.0	20.5	7.6	8.2	**15.0**	6.2	4.5	3.1
High	36.2	18.5	7.8	8.7	**14.6**	5.4	5.2	3.6

Cho (2013) argues that the negative effects of cyberbullying are more severe than traditional bullying. This is because of the unique characteristics of cyberbullying. Since it is not possible to directly check the victim's response in real time, the cyberbullies are more likely to repeatedly and more severely harass the victims. Second, cyberbullying can be more traumatic because it spreads very quickly. In the case of anonymous bullies, the victim may experience complex feelings of anger and anxiety (Hinduja and Patchin, 2009).

Short history of incidents in Japan

Bullying, cyberbullying, and Internet-mediated problems are sometimes overlapped or sequential in Japanese schools. Here, we will provide a short history of *ijime* (Japanese word for bullying) problems and then will consider how cyberbullying and other Internet-mediated incidents are plotted alongside that timeline. *ijime* was formerly used combined with *yowai-mono* which means weak people. So, *yowai-mono-ijime* meant bullying against weak people. As such, nowadays *ijime* still implies a power imbalance between victims and perpetrators. To understand in more detail, we can see the nuance of *ijime* in comparison to similar words in other countries (Smith et al., 2002).

In 1986, Japanese society was shaken by the news of the suicide of a Japanese 8th grade boy who had been bullied, not only by his peers but also by his three teachers. They bullied him, for example, by writing goodbye messages on a card and placing it on the boy's desk with a flower vase in the classroom, which indicated a "mock funeral". It was followed by his real one. When he committed suicide, he left the names of the perpetrators, so they were arrested and tried, and the school was found guilty.

In subsequent years, the amount of bullying noticed by teachers decreased and the media focus and public interest turned to school absenteeism. However, it was only the visibility of *ijime* that had changed, and the second media focus on *ijime* occurred in 1994, when a 14-year-old boy committed suicide. It stemmed from crime rather than trouble in school, as the perpetrators had extorted more than one million Japanese yen from the victim while severely harming him physically, and finally they were arrested. The third wave of media focus happened in 2006–2007 in reports of sequential *ijime* suicides. Most media criticised the schools and local educational committees, which placed additional stress on schools and teachers.

In 2011–2012, the *ijime* suicide case of an 8th grade boy in Otsu city, located in the Kansai area, resulted in media attention and became a major social issue. The school and the local Board of Education were blamed for not dealing with the bullying incidents properly and not reporting it sufficiently. Reacting to the enormous wave of social concern, the Japanese government implemented an Act requiring schools to be well-prepared to prevent and handle *ijime* incidents. In 2013, the Bullying Prevention Promotion Act (Ijime Boushi Taisaku Suishin Hou) came into force in September.

In 2016, a 14-year-old girl committed suicide in Kobe, and in 2018 it was revealed that a memorandum detailing the girl's relationships and events around her suicide elicited from students just after the incident had been concealed by the principal of the junior high school and a member of the local Board of Education. The Act requires local Boards of Education and schools to define and announce their policy on preventing and dealing with bullying.

However, when co-author of this chapter, Yuichi Toda, inquired at training courses whether schools were revising their policies, some of them answered that they had simply copied and pasted policies from somewhere, and most of them said they had not discussed the content with new students and their parents at the beginning of each school year. While some municipalities are aware of the importance of following the Act and not only revising their policies but supporting schools in detecting and dealing with incidents in their early stages, others are too far behind to follow the Act sufficiently.

Recently, in 2019, some issues were discussed concerning the amendment of the Bullying Prevention Promotion Act. Among them, the biggest issue was whether teachers who were unable to notice and cope with a case of severe bullying in their classes should be disciplined by law. A non-profit organisation called the "Gentle Heart Project", whose members are mostly parents who have lost their children due to bullying and other school incidents, held a meeting at a parliament. The purpose of the meeting was to argue for the necessity of such an amendment in order to improve teachers' attitude against bullying. It was at one stage on the lists of amendments, but it was later withdrawn due to strong objections from education sectors. There has been further discussion, and at the time of writing, their argument is ongoing.

Turning to cyberbullying in Japan, social concern began to arise around the mid-2000s. A search in the "CiNii" database in Japan suggests that the first publication with "cyberbullying" in its title was published in 2007. In the same year, the monthly journal *Education and Medicine* published a special issue on "The new threat: cyberbullying".

Tagawa (2012) conducted a qualitative analysis of newspaper articles and elicited five aspects of discourse on cyberbullying: 1) the increasing, more vicious and serious nature of cyberbullying; 2) the various avenues of cyberbullying (through anonymous websites on school matters, personal websites, SNS, and movie-sharing); 3) that anyone can be perpetrators or victims; 4) that it is difficult to find; and 5) that we should protect children from cyberbullying. Following the qualitative analysis, Tagawa (2019) conducted a quantitative text analysis on 279 Japanese newspaper articles, and depicted changes in the constellation and co-occurrence relationships in cyberbullying discourses. The results of the analysis are as follows. In the past, the term "mobile phone" was frequent, but after 2014 it no longer came out on top. The term "smartphone" now replaces the term "mobile phone". The term "underground school website" stopped appearing after 2011. Cyberbullying discourse is now often referred to as "trouble" and the discourse has changed from the underground school website to LINE (a communication app which is widely used in Japan) and other SNS.

In addition to such concerns about traditional bullying and cyberbullying, children face various kinds of problems related to the Internet, and social awareness and concerns about these problems have been growing. Chiba, Fujimura, and Takahashi (2009) report trends and studies on problems caused by illegal and harmful information on the Internet, which has come to be an important social problem in terms of public policy and child protection. They focused on problems such as dating sites, pro-suicide websites, internet child pornography distribution, cyberbullying, and threatening to commit a crime on the Internet.

When co-author Toda was a child, children were told that they "shouldn't go anywhere with unknown male adults", but nowadays, the media reports murder incidents of girls who were killed by adult males after being groomed via the Internet. In Japan, we do not have a similar word or phrase equivalent to "grooming", which may show our insufficient efforts to tackle such problems.

Culturally specific aspects of problems

Problems such as bullying, cyberbullying, addiction, and other Internet-mediated problems in Eastern countries do not seem much different from those of Western countries. But there are actually many differences. In addition, problems differ between South Korea and Japan. In this section we will analyse these differences using Western/Eastern and South Korean/Japanese comparisons.

In comparing bullying in the Western context and *ijime* in Japan, preserving comparability (i.e. measurement invariance) is necessary. However, it is possible that researchers skip some items which represent culturally specific ways of bullying. For example, Professor Dagmar Strohmeier and Toda once omitted some items from their own lists, as they felt that those items would only be relevant in Japan (and not in Austria).

Item 1. How often have you been left out on purpose when it was time to play or do an activity?
Item 2. How often has someone suddenly stopped talking and stayed silent when you approached them?
Item 3. How often has someone treated you as if you were not there?

These three items are mainly asking about invisible bullying in relationships, which may be more common in Japan than in Austria. Perpetrators ignore the victim, concealing their intention. That's why in the actual situation, it is very difficult to detect this kind of *ijime*, and teachers can not intervene by just watching the children. Though the teachers point out that the behaviours are regarded as *ijime*, the perpetrators can say that was just a coincidence without harmful intentions.

With regards to cyberbullying, Ono and Saito (2018) classify cyberbullying from the Japanese viewpoint into three types: message type, web-board type, and group type. From a South Korean viewpoint, such classification is both similar and different. Both countries suffer from group-type cyberbullying, but the difference is in how it damages the victims. The Japanese way is termed "LINE Hazushi" (exclusion from LINE group) and the South Korean way is termed "Kakao Talk Prison". LINE is the most commonly used messenger app in Japan, while Kakao Talk is the most popular messenger app in Korea.

LINE Hazushi is one of the typical ways of exclusion in cyberspace in Japan while Kakao Talk Prison is one of the typical ways of attacking in cyberspace in South Korea. Interestingly, we haven't heard of the Japanese way of cyberbullying in South Korea, and vice versa. As far as we are aware there is no Kakao Talk Prison in Japan and no LINE Hazushi in South Korea. Ono and Saito (2018) conducted and evaluated social skills training to cope with LINE Hazushi, which leaves somebody out of a LINE group. LINE Hazushi refers to making a new subgroup to exclude a certain person from the previous group. To explain it in a more concrete way, let's name the original LINE group as "group A", the excluded person as "S", and the new LINE group as "Group A-S". This means there are two LINE groups which are mostly made up of the same members, and the difference is whether it is "with S" or "without S". Perpetrators can keep Group A to pretend they are good friends to S (sometimes S does not know the existence of Group A-S), but in Group A-S they are chatting negatively about S. In other cases, perpetrators can ignore Group A without any reaction and S will soon notice their exclusion. In the former case, the perpetrators enjoy the process of being noticed gradually by S, by saying something that S does not know due to S's exclusion from Group A-S.

On the contrary, in South Korea, Kakao Talk Prison is not like LINE Hazushi. Kakao Talk Prison is used by perpetrators as a group to verbally abuse one victim in the group. When the victim leaves a group chat room, the term "prison" is used because perpetrators invite the victim back again and continue to verbally abuse the victim. It is a continuous shower of negative messages against a victim in a group. The term "prison" represents its state which does not allow the victim to escape from it. In addition, if the victim blocks the other person's verbal attack, the perpetrators use different accounts to invite the victim. Therefore, the victim feels imprisoned and suffers from severe psychological pain. LINE Hazushi harasses the victim with a cover-up of who the perpetrator is, while Kakao Talk Prison is different in that it reveals who the perpetrators are. With LINE Hazushi, the perpetrators enjoy gossiping or mocking the victim after excluding the victim. This type of bullying is also a way to make the victim feel pain by letting the victim find him/herself ostracised and ridiculed. Therefore, it is a way of bullying using relational aggression. Kakao Talk Prison, on the other hand, takes a more direct and open approach to attack. This is a way for the group to cohere and use their collective power to harass the victim directly, regardless of what the perpetrators themselves are exposed to.

Other cultural differences may exist and in the future new varieties may emerge like the differences introduced above. We should keep in mind that such differences exist, and our strategies should tackle problems considering such differences. And that's why we should be careful in implementing prevention measures which were developed in other cultural backgrounds.

Cultural backgrounds

Our discussions about cyberbullying and Internet-mediated problems in Eastern countries allow us to see how these issues appear in a modern society with Information and Communications Technology alongside still-strong cultural backgrounds. Some studies have focused on the relationship between cultural values and bullying. Georgiou and colleagues (2013) found that bullying is related to cultural values (individualism vs. collectivism). Huang, Hong, and Espelage (2013) also stressed the importance of considering the impact of cultural factors from an ecological perspective when understanding bullying in Asian countries. For example, the ecological system framework of Bronfenbrenner highlights the effects of collectivism and individualism, corresponding to macro systems, on bullying. In Japan and South Korea bullying is often considered to occur collectively because of their culture. However, nowadays such cultural impacts are mixed due to the borderless exchanges of literature, movies, communications, and so on, and the moving and migrating of people. We have to consider such circumstances when we see the problems among children and plan the implementation of countermeasures.

Collectivism

Some people argue that collectivism in Eastern countries, especially Japan, is a factor in bullying. However, Takano (2019) thoroughly examined the wealth of literature and warned that it was not adequate to regard the Japanese as collectivistic, and the view was merely a cultural stereotype. Here, we do not discuss this argument in detail, but we can say at least that though both South Korea and Japan are considered to be collective cultures by some people, there are substantial cultural differences between those two countries.

In Japan, when a school-bullying incident receives wide media coverage, the school involved is often overwhelmed by anonymous phone calls. These calls, paradoxically, might be seen to have similarities to the school bullying they relate to. People who ring and talk in a punitive way may think they are correcting the schools. However, such a large volume of phone calls, and their anonymous nature, merely provide obstacles for the school to cope with the ongoing problem. In addition, nowadays it is possible to search for private information about the reported perpetrator's family; this is often shared online and leads to the family being subjected to an enormous volume of unpleasant phonecalls, suspicious post, and so on. Sometimes, the private information is wrong or misleading and such collective "justice" turns out to be injustice.

In South Korea, collective culture affects bullying. The annual survey on school violence shows a very high rate of collective violence. The rate of verbal violence was the highest in frequency of violence, followed by collective violence, accounting for 23.2 percent of the total violence. This figure represents a 6 percent increase from the previous year (Ministry of Education, 2019), suggesting collective violence is increasing year on year. One interesting notion about *wang-ta*, known as Korean bullying, is that the official term for *wang-ta* is "collective bullying". Since *wang-ta* is regarded as slang, the term "collective bullying" has been used in official documents. Oh (2010) argued that the use of the term "group bullying" in Korea, compared to "bullying" in Western countries, reflects Korea's collectivistic culture. When the term *wang-ta* was coined in the middle of 1990s, the phenomenon of collective bullying was prominent.

Collective moral disengagement

People sometimes ignore social rules which they know and they can follow. At the beginning of the research on such processes, nowadays named "moral disengagement", Bandura (1986) described it as a selective dis-functioning mechanism of the self-regulatory process. Recently, "collective moral disengagement" (Gini, Pozzoli, and Bussey, 2014) has become well known and referred to in attempts to understand bullying. Our question here is whether collective moral disengagement is similar or different in Eastern countries and what kind of factors may determine the selective process of moral disengagement. If we can see "collectivism" in Eastern culture, might this enhance "collective" moral disengagement? And furthermore, a collective situation may be related to a situation of anonymity, as situations that preserve anonymity may enhance collective behaviours, and collective situations with huge numbers of people may help individuals remain anonymous. Collectivism is not directly related to the collective situation, but if collectivism appears in such a situation, collectivistic cultures are somewhat problematic, as this enhances anonymity which might lead to moral disengagement. These ideas will be explored in more detail in Chapter 8.

Investigating relationships among collectivism, collective situation, anonymity, and collective moral disengagement are beyond the focus of this book, and have not yet been the subject of research, but we would like to keep this question in mind when arguing about Eastern culture, problems with bullying, and countermeasures.

Hon-ne *and* tatemae

To explain moral disengagement in Japan and the exclusion type of *ijime*, the Japanese words *hon-ne* and *tatemae* should be introduced. *Hon-ne* refers to a person's true feelings or thoughts, while *tatemae* refers to the feelings or thoughts that someone presents in public. People use *tatemae* to avoid unexpected conflict with others; sometimes they tell *hon-ne* to only their limited intimate friends and family. If there is a big discrepancy between *tatemae* and *hon-ne* and the *hon-ne* was told without/with intention, such a situation will bring considerable harm to the recipient. The person cannot believe the big discrepancy between *tatemae* and *hon-ne*, and may be very distressed. One extreme example appeared in a scenario which was written by Japanese junior high school students who showed their play to other students and teachers (Takeuchi, 2011). In the scenario, a girl was suffering from cyberbullying, but her close friend supported her and helped her get through it. The bullying continued as if the perpetrator knew every aspect of the victim's feelings. At last, the close friend coldly revealed that the perpetrator was herself.

Sawada (2014) presents bullying as a "dark side of adaptation", taking into account the role of personality to handle the imbalance of internal and external aspects. Here, Sawada (2014) refers to traditional double viewpoints on adaptation: the internal aspect of adaptation related to self-evaluation measured by self-esteem and sense of authenticity and the external aspect of meeting the demands and expectations from the environment such as consideration for others and relational maintenance. Thus his argument focuses on personality and its related concepts in describing an imbalanced state of those internal and external aspects of adaptation, defining "over-adaptation" as de-valuing the internal aspects and over-valuing the external aspects.

Such a complex view is not easy to apply to understand and tackle the problems we discuss here. However, we should be careful to keep in mind the fact that people appear differently in various occasions and sometimes hide their thoughts and emotions. And such tendencies would be considerably influenced by cultural backgrounds.

In Korea, there are no official terms like *hon-ne* and *tatemae*. However, Korean culture also values recognition of others, so people are often sensitive to social recognition and act up to other people's expectations rather than what they want. Western people tend to regulate social behaviour with guilt, so schools create and enforce strict regulation. Students are socialised to feel bad or have a guilty conscience about bullying behaviours (Bedford and Hwang, 2003). On the other hand, Eastern people regulate their behaviour with shame, so public opinions are critical in determining what is right and wrong. Thus, students tend to use more invisible types of bullying such as relational and social bullying, because visible types of bullying such as physical bullying can easily reveal their misbehaviour and consequently cause them to feel ashamed.

Guidelines for effective interventions

Considering the cultural differences in bullying discussed in this chapter, here we discuss themes which will help in guiding the development of culturally relevant interventions. In later chapters, it will be important to consider these themes when looking at countermeasures such as apps, manga, and anime.

Appropriateness of the scenarios

Alongside the development of SNS, new ways of bullying and new types of problems are appearing among children, so it would not be relevant to keep using old scenarios when we discuss problems with children. We need to renew the scenarios to catch up with the actual lives of children. However, if the way of bullying or type of problem we present is only beginning to appear among children, the scenario might provide inappropriate information for children. To avoid these kinds of adverse effects, we should be aware of children's experience and carefully nurture their basic attitude to such problems.

For example, Kanetsuna and Toda (2017) reported on a project conducted at a junior high school in Hyogo Prefecture. The project was a student-led approach in which actual activities within the school were mostly conducted by the student committee. The students first collected opinions on *ijime* from their peers in order to understand their general perceptions of *ijime*, and then produced video footage for anti-*ijime* awareness-raising with English and Japanese subtitles, so that it could be distributed all over the world (www.youtube.com/watch?v=ZW92_9SYb-0). In the scenario, the teachers/researchers who supported them were considering giving lectures to children to explain the research framework for bullying, especially regarding types of bullying. However, the adults did not tell students about "knowledge" such as physical, verbal, and indirect ways of bullying. As a result, students did not create vignettes reflecting such typologies, but instead showed their own ideas. Their three stories introduced how *ijime* may have unintentional beginnings. What started as just misunderstandings or jokes were gradually becoming serious and severe, and eventually including enough aggression to be seen as *ijime*. Such stories wouldn't have come up if students started writing scenarios after lectures by adult experts.

Awareness of not being anonymous

Though it is difficult to say whether the Internet is anonymous or not, it is clear that most children using the Internet are not anonymous. Probably not knowing or ignoring this fact, most children are using SNS. Most do not know how dangerous it is to be connected to someone in SNS that they do not know; others are seeking someone to talk with despite suspecting the risks. In addition, children can act as perpetrators or offenders without knowing it is possible to be detected as an actor. When children do know that they are not anonymous in SNS, their behaviour norms are similar to their usual norms in face-to-face daily life.

Toda (2013) introduced a lesson by Mr. Aoya which focuses on the problem of anonymity. Mr. Aoya, a school teacher, developed a lesson with his colleagues to let students consider the importance of being aware of whether they are "anonymous or not anonymous". He first showed a written sample dialogue of an interviewer and an athlete from the Internet. The athlete derogates sports without professional leagues, saying that it is ridiculous to put so much effort into something that will neither make any money nor lead to a future career. Then, Mr. Aoya asked students to write down what they think about the athlete's opinion and to put their names on the top of the sheet. After writing their own opinions, students are shown some insulting messages which were actually written on the website following the sample dialogue. After identifying the differences between the comments made by the students and those on the website, students discussed the reasons for such differences. One of the most plausible answers was: "As they are writing on the web-page without their names". By comparing the comments, students identified how anonymity affects people's expression of opinions.

Conversion in how to see people's nature

As stated above, people usually conceal *hon-ne* to avoid bad reactions from others, but if they regard themselves to be safe in a situation because they can hide themselves anonymously, they may be reluctant to keep *tatemae*.

In Mr. Aoya's class introduced above, after students noticed the difference between the comments, another idea developed. At first, students thought that the people who had written nasty comments on the website against the athlete were nasty people. However, they then realised that the students themselves might write the same kind of nasty comments on the website if they were reading the dialogue and believed that they could write anything anonymously. This might have led to a conversion of their views about the unknown people. The seemingly nasty people on the website may actually be ordinary people as they themselves are, if they were to meet each other off-line.

This meant that sometimes *tatemae* conceals *hon-ne*, and sometimes "nasty comments" hide "ordinary characters". In usual classes for reading or moral education, such conversion has been tried by teachers. Novels and TV dramas also offer such conversion stories to children. However, we suspect it is difficult in our daily life to bring such conversions to our way of looking at other people. And of course, while it would be not easy, it would be worth trying to develop apps that could develop such conversions on how to see other people's nature.

Overview of the following chapters

Chapter 2 introduces theories and research in traditional/cyberbullying and Internet-mediated problems in Japan and South Korea. With regard to South Korean research trends, it is based on the ecological model by Bronfenbrenner. Problems are of course rooted in individual thoughts and tendencies but at the same time, such variables are influenced by family and social factors. Most of the mechanisms are similar to those in Western countries, but there are some subtle differences that are important to consider in order to detect problems and provide better countermeasures. With regard to Japanese research trends, the framework will be models concerning the structure and process of *ijime*. Such models inform us that *ijime* is not a phenomenon among just perpetrators and victims, but a complex process involving reinforcers and onlookers who differ in their thoughts and behaviours. Also the process model tells us that *ijime* is a phenomenon which is gradually constructed and worsened by the growing number of perpetrators. Such notions are inevitable to tackle the problem. Studies on Internet addiction and other related problems are also introduced.

Chapter 3 presents a new "Level of Immersion in Media Experience (LIME) model" which is a framework to categorise countermeasures using manga, apps, and games. The model distinguishes the level of immersion according to the type of the media and its system, which may set the basic level of the immersion of children.

Chapter 4 focuses on the impact of manga on children. Visual media such as manga, anime, and games are very popular among children not only in Japan, but also in other countries. Although such pop cultures have achieved widespread popularity worldwide, little is known about their impact on children. In particular, positive aspects are not well discussed. Therefore, it is necessary to investigate the significance of their popularity and possible impact on children. This chapter discusses the following three points: 1) the reason children are devoted to manga, 2) impact of manga on children, and 3) positive use of manga to prevent traditional/cyberbullying and other Internet-related problems.

Chapter 5 is also theoretical and discusses effective approaches to utilising games and apps to prevent traditional bullying and cyberbullying. Compared to traditional approaches of reducing bullying through verbal instruction, games and apps have a variety of advantages such as being more interactive, fun, and interesting. This chapter will look at what types of games and apps have been developed to enhance coping strategies for bullying. It introduces how the games and apps help potential victims to enhance their coping strategies. It explains how students learn more effectively by games and apps compared to traditional interventions. This chapter will provide a theoretical foundation and literature review in order to show the effectiveness of games and apps.

Chapter 6 introduces a case study on the development of a serious game called "Angry Daddy". This game was designed for middle school students to increase their coping skills when they were verbally attacked in cyberspace. The game players learn how to react better in virtual chat-like conversations. The chapter discusses the detailed procedure of developing this serious game, including concept design, creation of core content, and utilisation of a feedback system. Both qualitative and quantitative research methods were used to evaluate the effectiveness of the game. Based on the analysis of the game design and its educational effectiveness, several factors are suggested for the effective design of an anti-cyberbullying educational game. This research is expected to be helpful for the future design of educational games.

Chapter 7 introduces two anti-bullying apps which have been widely used in Korea. The first is "117 Chat" which is a secured reporting app for students to notify a school police officer about a bullying situation. It also provides victims with 24-hour chatting services. The second is the "Cyberbullying Vaccine" in which people virtually experience cyberbullying as victims, so that they recognise the significant impact of cyberbullying. This chapter introduces the characteristics, effectiveness, and limitations of the two anti-bullying smartphone apps.

Chapter 8 introduces Japanese prevention practices which are challenging moral disengagement caused by anonymity. One such practice used in schools in Japan is the Internet-based set of teaching materials named "Jotore", which provides children with an opportunity for learning, sharing, and experiencing various online literacy and morals in a safe and friendly way. One of the features of this "Jotore" is dedicated to helping children learn about the non-anonymity of the Internet and its incompleteness. This chapter introduces and examines various prevention and intervention practices to tackle the belief of anonymity, including both class lessons and practices using pc games and apps in Japan for on- and off-line bullying and other childhood misbehaviour.

Chapters 9, 10, and 11 are commentary chapters by authors with Western and other Asian cultural backgrounds. Chapter 9 is a commentary piece on the previous chapters based on the insights of researchers in Thailand, who have been contributing to worldwide collaborations to tackle traditional/cyberbullying. In Thailand, cyberbullying research and online safety workshops are already emerging, however laws, policies, and programs should be progressed more in the future. The applicability and suitability of some of the solutions in previous chapters in the Thai context are discussed.

Chapter 10 is based in Norway, written by an established researcher in the use of digital technologies by young children. The author has visited Japan several times, and even published a collection of poems that connect Japanese words to rich metaphors. In this commentary chapter, she summarises the broader themes in the eight chapters of the volume and reflects on the lessons learned and lessons to be learned in the study of cyberbullying and young children. She begins her account with a short expose of her professional background and connection to this research theme, followed by some observations on the topics examined by the book's authors. She concludes with some recommendations for future work in the area.

Chapter 11 is based in North America. As professors who actively investigate and write about bullying, the authors describe the value of the book from a cross-cultural perspective. They discuss the possibilities and limitations of the various methods presented in this book and offer practical suggestions for further research.

References

Bandura, A. (1986). *Social Foundations of Thought and Action: A Social Cognitive Theory.* Englewood Cliffs, NJ: Prentice-Hall.

Bedford, O. and Hwang, K. K. (2003). Guilt and shame in Chinese culture: A cross-cultural framework from the perspective of morality and identity. *Journal for the Theory of Social Behaviour, 33*(2), 127–144. doi:10.1111/1468–5914.00210

Chiba, N., Fujimura, A., and Takahashi, K. (2009). Latest trends and studies of some problems that caused by illegal and harmful information on the Internet. *IPSJ SIG Technical Reports, 44*, 115–120.

Cho, Y. O. (2013). The impact of cyber bullying victim experience and the influence of mediating effect of depression on delinquent behaviors. *Korean Journal of Youth Studies, 20*(10), 117–142.

Georgiou, S. N., Fousiani, K., Michaelides, M., and Stavrinides, P. (2013). Cultural value orientation and authoritarian parenting as parameters of bullying and victimization at school. *International Journal of Psychology, 48*(1), 69–78. doi:10.1080/00207594.2012.754104

Gini, G., Pozzoli, T., and Bussey, K. (2014). Collective moral disengagement: Initial validation of a scale for adolescents. *European Journal of Developmental Psychology, 11*(3), 386–395. doi:10.1080/17405629.2013.851024

Hinduja, S. and Patchin, J. W. (2009). Cyberbullying research summary: Emotional and psychological consequences. *Cyberbullying Research Center*, 1–2.

Huang, H., Hong, J. S., and Espelage, D. L. (2013). Understanding factors associated with bullying and peer victimization in Chinese schools within ecological contexts. *Journal of Child and Family Studies, 22*(7), 881–892. doi:10.1007/s10826-012-9647-4

Kanetsuna, T. and Toda, Y. (2017). Applying multiple indices to monitor bullying longitudinally: A case of a Japanese junior high school. *Psychological Test and Assessment Modeling, 59*, 135–156.

Koo, H. J., Kwak, K. J., and Smith, P. (2008). Victimization in Korean schools: The nature, incidence, and distinctive features of Korean bullying or Wang-Ta. *Journal of School Violence, 7*(4), 119–139. doi:10.1080/15388220801974084

Lee, D. H. (2014). Conceptualization and self-report assessment of school bullying: Current issues and future directions. *The Korean Journal of Psychology: General, 33*(4), 759–788.

Ministry of Education (2014a). *Guidebook Handling Issues of School Violence.* Korean Ministry of Education & Institute of School Violence Prevention.

Ministry of Education (2014b). *The Second Student Survey Result on School Violence in 2013.* Korean Ministry of Education.

Ministry of Education (2019). *The First Student Survey Result on School Violence in 2019.* Korean Ministry of Education.

Oh, I. (2010). School counselor's whole-school approach to school bullying. *The Korean Journal of Counseling, 11*(1), 303–316. doi:10.15703/kjc.11.1.201003.303

Ono, A. and Saito, F. (2018). Social skill training on leaving somebody out of a LINE group. *Senri Kinran University Bulletin, 15*, 15–22.

Sainio, M., Herkama, S., Kontio, M., and Salmivalli, C. (2019). KiVa Anti-Bullying Program. In P. K. Smith (ed.), *Making an Impact on School Bullying: Interventions and Recommendations* (pp. 45–66). New York: Routledge.

Salmivalli, C. and Poskiparta, E. (2012). Making bullying prevention a priority in Finnish schools: The KiVa antibullying program. *New Directions for Youth Development, 2012*(133), 41–53. doi:10.1002/yd.20006

Sawada, M. (2014). Balance between private and public selves: Trends in personality research on adaptation. *The Annual Report of Educational Psychology in Japan, 53*, 37–49. doi:10.5926/arepj.53.37

Smith, P. K., Cowie, H., Olafsson, R. F., and Liefooghe, A. (2002). Definitions of bullying: A comparison of terms used, and age and gender differences, in a fourteen-country international comparison. *Child Development, 73*, 1119–1133. doi:10.1111/1467–8624.00461

Song, J. Y. and Oh, I. S. (2015). A comparison analysis of self-report and peer-nomination in the assessment of school violence. *Korean Journal of Counseling, 16*(4), 377–394. doi:10.15703/kjc.16.4.201508.377

Tagawa, T. (2019). Changes in the constellation and co-occurrence relationships in cyberbullying discourses: Quantitative text analysis of newspaper articles. *Journal of Chubu University Liberal Arts, 1*, 1–13.

Tagawa, T. (2012). Characteristics of cyberbullying discourse: From analysis on newspaper articles. *Journal of Nagoya Bunri University, 12*, 89–95.

Takano, Y. (2019). *Dangerous Mistake in an Argument on Japanese People: Temptation and Trap of Cultural Stereotype*. Tokyo: Discover21.

Takeuchi, K. (2011). Children's own initiative to change their school: A glimmer of hope after a tragic incident. In R. H. Shute, P. T. Slee, R. Murray-Harvey, and K. L. Dix (eds.), *Mental Health and Wellbeing: Educational Perspectives* (pp. 347–350). Adelaide, South Australia: Shannon Research Press.

Toda, Y. (2013). Bullying research and supporting prevention practices in schools. *Japanese Journal of Developmental Psychology, 24*, 460–470. doi:10.11201/jjdp.24.460

2 Theories and research on traditional/cyberbullying and Internet-mediated problems

Yuichi Toda, Insoo Oh, Toshiro Tsuruta, and Tomoyuki Kanetsuna

There has been a long research tradition on *wang-ta* in Korea and *ijime* in Japan. In addition, in recent decades, new problems of cyberbullying and other Internet-mediated problems including Internet addiction, inappropriate posting, flaming, and so on have been issues of concern. While most children and adolescents enjoy the convenience and entertainment of the Internet and smartphones, a noticeable number of them are ignorant about the risks in using such services. In this chapter, we start by providing an overview of research on traditional school bullying and its related problems in South Korea and Japan.

Not only do the problems that we observe in each country vary, but also the frameworks in which research is located. South Korean research on *wang-ta* is explained in terms of the framework of Bronfenbrenner's Ecological Systems Theory (Bronfenbrenner, 1979). While this model can be applicable to locate Japanese research of *ijime*, it seems Japanese studies are instead much more narrowly focused on *ijime* in schools. In terms of cyberbullying, viewpoints of both countries look similar but not yet fixed as the problems continue to grow and change. For the other Internet-mediated problems, studies in both countries are still at an early stage and we need further investigations in this area.

Korean research on traditional/cyberbullying and Internet-mediated problems

Korean research on school bullying

Among various theoretical explanations of school bullying, the most comprehensive one is ecological systems theory. Bronfenbrenner's ecological systems theory states that social behaviours of children and adolescents depend on not only their individual characteristics, but also how various systemic factors interact in the bigger social context. Therefore, it emphasises that the harm that students experience from bullying is affected by the interaction in the broader social context of factors such as individual characteristics, school and local communities, family background, and cultural contexts. That is, the risk factors are created by the interaction between the ecosystems of microsystem, mesosystem, exosystem, and macrosystem (Lee and Oh, 2012).

Self-esteem, empathy, and aggression are the factors most frequently studied in individual characteristics. Self-esteem has mainly been studied in victims. The self-esteem of victims was found to be consistently lower than that of those who are not bullied (Choi, 2006). In contrast, there have been inconsistent findings about bullies' self-esteem. For example, in several studies, the self-esteem of bullies has been shown to be higher than that of non-bullies (Lee and Kwak, 2000), while other studies have found the opposite (H. H. Kim, 2002; Kwon and Kim, 2009; Lee and Kim, 2000).

Empathy has mainly been studied in bullies, with studies finding that bullies have lower empathy levels than other students (Shin, 2012). However, some studies distinguished empathy into cognitive empathy and emotional empathy and examined the difference between the two types of empathy (Ghim, 2012). While cognitive empathy is related to the ability to understand how painful victimized students would feel, emotional empathy is related to the ability to 'feel' the pain that the victims experienced on a similar level. Such studies suggest that students are more likely to bully others when emotional empathy is lacking rather than cognitive empathy. Therefore, Oh (2010) emphasised that any intervention intending to decrease bullying behaviours by enhancing the empathy of bullies would not be effective if it only focused on cognitive empathy.

Aggression is known as the most powerful factor in predicting perpetration of bullying (Li and Oh, 2017). Some studies have separated aggression into two types: proactive and reactive. Proactive aggression can be defined as acting forcefully – domination and aggressiveness – in order to attain what one desires, without any recognised threat to oneself. On the other hand, reactive aggression appears when one shows aggressive behaviours as a response to a recognised threat, that is, only if others threaten or attack. Lee and her colleagues (2014) categorised elementary students into four groups to compare their aggression: bullies, victims, bully-victims, and non-involved students. Based on answers to a questionnaire, they reported that bullies showed high proactive aggression while bully-victims showed high reactive aggression. From these results, Lee and her colleagues argued that if victims have high reactive aggression, in response to being bullied, they are highly likely to become bully-victims eventually by attacking the bullies or others.

The microsystems of family, peers, and schools are known factors which affect school bullying. These three microsystems have a direct interaction with students; students from highly dysfunctional families, having many aggressive peers, and attending schools with an accepting atmosphere to violence are known to show a high degree of bullying. Family may work as a risk factor or a protective factor for bullying in various forms. If the parenting method is authoritative, children are more likely to be bullies (Lee, 2004), and children who grow up watching their parents being frequently violent are also more likely to be bullies (Kim, 2014). In particular, attachment to parents is known to affect children's bullying (Hong, 2016). If children have unstable attachments with their parents, they are more likely to show aggressive behaviour. However, the family may work as a protective factor in bullying as well. Lee and Kim (2012) explored protective factors at the family level affecting the adaptation of bullied adolescents through a longitudinal analysis. Bullied victims who had stable attachments to their parents and siblings, with solid protective factors quickly adapted emotionally and socially at school. Seo and Choi (2016) also found that students with higher family resilience experience less anxiety in situations where their social anxiety increased due to the experience of being bullied.

Studies that have analysed peer influence also show the effect of the peer system on bullying, with a significant effect of friends' delinquency on bullying behaviours (Do and Lee, 2009). Shin (2015) used longitudinal social network analysis to study the tendency of preferring peers with similar behaviour characteristics as themselves. The analysis confirmed that students with friends who show a high tendency toward school violence are also likely to show a higher degree of bullying themselves.

The school system is also thought to have an effect on the levels of bullying. The main finding is that when class cohesiveness is higher, there is a greater buffer to the negative effects of bullying (Kim and Ko, 2014). Victims often isolate themselves from the community because of their bad memories of social relationships and, then, experience psychological shock due to decreased social support. If class cohesiveness is higher, the social support among peers increases, buffering psychological shock. Also, at the school level, school atmosphere (Kim and Moon, 2016) and the characteristics of the school system (Kim, 2007) are proven to have effects on bullying. For example, in schools with a more democratic school atmosphere – how well teachers and students interact, how well the school policies are consistently enforced, how actively students participate in school policies – bullying behaviours are found to be inhibited.

The mesosystem is based on the interconnections between two or more microsystems (Bronfenbrenner, 1994). Therefore, bullying is affected by two different subsystems interacting. Park (2017) found that bullied students have lower levels of subjective happiness, and that support from friends, family, and teachers mediates between the experience of being bullied and subjective happiness. This indicates that once you have been bullied, you are likely to have less social support from friends, family, and teachers, which eventually leads to lower levels of happiness. This result shows that the support system of peers, family, and school mediates the relationship between a victim's experiences and their happiness. Kim and Moon (2016) also found that school atmosphere and family communication affect both bullies and victims. In this study, students in a negative school atmosphere and from a family that does not have effective communication show higher anxiety about being bullied and are actually more likely either to be bullied or to bully others. It demonstrates that characteristics of the family system and school affect bullying. Kim, Chung, and Lee (2008) also found that adolescents were not involved in bullying behaviours if they had strong support from peers or teachers, despite their exposure to their parents' domestic violence. Their findings support the idea of interactions between a child's family and peers/schools.

The exosystem is composed of different areas that do not directly influence the individual, but where events do occur, they indirectly affect one's life (Bronfenbrenner, 1994). Several studies have found that violent content on mass media influences individuals' bullying behaviours. According to Kim and Kim's findings (2018) from a meta-analysis on factors causing bullying behaviours, exposure to violent content on the media and in the social setting, and a harmful environment surrounding the schools and local communities are shown to affect bullying behaviours significantly. Shin (2016), investigating the effect of each individual exosystem, found that the longer someone watches violent content, the more likely they are to commit school bullying and cyberbullying. In another study, exposure to media violence was highly correlated with the perpetration of school bullying while also moderating the relationship between aggression and bullying (Do, 2008). Kim (2006) also found that media violence was the strongest predictor of bullying among elementary school students.

The macrosystem is the cultural environment in which individuals live, and it is defined as customs, norms, and culture existing throughout the culture and subsystems (Bronfenbrenner, 1994). Kang (2012) pointed out in her qualitative study that violent adolescent group culture causes bullying by exploring the context and the process of bullying. That culture, which shows a clear, strict power structure in the peer group alongside weak character education, worsens the power imbalance existing between bullies and victims. Lee and Kim (2001) pointed out that students are more likely to be bullied when they do not conform to the norms in that group; in middle school, the power structure existing among students is relatively clear, and if they do not follow such norms, they are more likely to get bullied. The academic-centred culture created by the curriculum in Korea also is related to bullying. Park (2006) suggests that students' aggressive behaviours may increase due to enhanced tension and a considerable amount of stress in pressured studying to attain high academic achievement. In fact, Kim and Moon (2016) found that students are more likely to experience being bullied and bullying when their academic stress is higher.

As examined so far, school bullying does not happen without a context; it rather results from complicated interactions between an individual and their family, peer group, school, local community, social norms, and so on. In other words, individual factors (aggression, self-esteem, empathy), family factors (proper supervision, abuse, or domestic violence), peer factors (acceptance of violence, group violence), school factors (negligence of school, negative atmosphere), and local community factors (aggression within the local community, lack of resources within the community, lack of solidarity between the local community and school) interact together in complicated ways to affect bullying.

Korean research on cyberbullying

Various theories are used as the conceptual frameworks in explaining cyberbullying. Classic theories include social learning theory, differential association theory, self-control theory, and general strain theory. Research on cyberbullying supporting each theory can be summarised as follows.

First, according to social learning theory, originally proposed by Bandura (1986), cyberbullying can be understood as a 'learned' phenomenon, because adolescents learn others' violent behaviours through observation or imitation online. Students may acquire new violent behaviour techniques by observing or imitating others' violent behaviours. Or they may imitate violent behaviours with no particular awareness or feelings of guilt. That is, those who experienced more violence at home, in school, or in society are more likely to be more aggressive and to perpetrate violence than those who do not. In fact, students who observed domestic violence are found to be more likely to participate in cyberbullying (K. E. Kim, 2012). Also, those who experienced offline bullying at school are more likely to participate in cyberbullying (Kim and Choi, 2017). In social learning theory, adolescents are understood to learn behaviours from interaction with others; their bigger exposure to violent behaviours in cyberspace leads them to learn cyberbullying behaviours. Therefore, exposure to violent behaviours may act as a risk factor according to social learning theory.

In fact, E. K. Kim (2012) showed that peer pressure and the number of friends who have taken part in online delinquency act as significant correlated factors of cyberbullying perpetration. Lee (2005) also proved that those who approached delinquent friends were more likely to act in cyberbullying. Additionally, in terms of verbal cyberbullying, the influence of violent friends was found to be significant. Among various factors, contact with delinquent friends seemed to have the biggest influence. Jun and Lee (2010) demonstrated that contact with friends who had taken part in online delinquency acted as the strongest influence in causing online delinquency. Chun and colleagues (2008) discovered that the more serious the violent behaviours of peer groups gets and the less they participate in cyber club activities working as their friend's support role, the more they perpetrate cyberbullying. Also, according to social learning theory, children may learn violent behaviours from violent content on TV, video media, cartoons, or books or may imitate violent actions from their parents or the older generation. Fanti and colleagues (2012) suggested that exposure to and learning violence through mass media may result in imitating violence and accepting such behaviours, which can affect the perpetration of cyberbullying.

Second, differential association theory explains that when adolescents are more closely connected to other adolescents' violent behaviours, they are more likely to perpetrate cyberbullying. That is, when adolescents perceive, from their interaction with the delinquency group, that aggressive behaviours can be rewarding, the likelihood of them perpetrating such violent behaviours increases. In many studies that investigated adolescent delinquencies or school violence, when students often interact with delinquent peer groups, they are more likely to participate in violent or delinquent behaviours (M. J. Kim, 2002; Cho, 2006; Lee, 2005). When adolescents are continuously exposed to environments that accept and justify violence, they accept it and learn it, which makes it easier for them to perpetrate violence on others; the more frequent their exposure to the violent environment is, the more likely they are to try violence or forceful measures in a conflict situation.

Sung and colleagues (2006) discovered that adolescents who experienced more cyberbullying as victims were more likely to turn into bullies. They were found to feel less guilty because they can justify their perpetration. That is, they learn violence through being bullied and it prepares their bullying of others. Adolescents today acquire information from cyberspace, and interact with one another in cyberspace rather than directly interacting with surrounding people, including their friends. Therefore, the effect of the Internet on their value systems and attitudes is huge. That is, applying differential association theory, not only interactions within the actual classroom but also their experiences in cyberspace may affect adolescents' cyberbullying behaviours.

Third, according to self-control theory (Gottfredson and Hirschi, 1990), cyberbullying occurs due to mis-control of immediate and momentary impulses. The theory suggests differences in the ability to control one's own aggression leads to whether a person perpetrates cyberbullying or not. Such self-control depends on the students' parents or caregivers' parenting style when the students were young. Therefore, if the students were neglected in an environment that lacked supervision or affection, they are more likely to have low self-control; they are more likely to bully others unexpectedly, as an impulse. In cyberspace, one often encounters various situations where one may express one's thoughts unexpectedly or impulsively; as such, here self-control can be considered extremely important as a control factor (Lee, 2007). That is, it is important to remember that children with low self-control within cyberspace are more likely to participate in bullying. Many previous studies suggest self-control as a risk factor related to perpetration of cyberbullying (Kim and Choi, 2012; E. K. Kim 2012; Jun and Lee, 2010; Cha, 2012; Hong and Kim, 2011). In E. K. Kim's findings (2012), self-control showed a more significant effect on cyberbullying in male students. Hong and Kim (2011) found that self-control indirectly affected female students in cyberbullying while examining how self-control and stress affected cyberbullying. Jun and Lee (2010) also found that aggression and low self-control are personal factors that cause group cyberbullying (when two or more bullies are attacking their victims online).

Korean research on Internet-mediated problems

Internet-mediated problems can be classified in various ways. Seo (2009) distinguished Internet-mediated problems into direct types (e.g., exposure to pornography, obscene chatting, computer virus spread, Internet gambling, and fraud) and indirect types (e.g., absence or skipping classes due to over-indulgence in Internet). Jue and Kwon (2001) classified various problem behaviours related to the Internet into three different types. Three main functions of Internet – providing information, communication, and entertainment – are used as criteria. Problems related to information were shown as spreading harmful information or illegal use of personal information. Regarding the communication function, students showed aggressive behaviour on the Internet, exploited financial benefits, or stalked others. In terms of the entertainment function, students showed addictive behaviour in games, gambling, or sexual stimulation. Despite these classifications, most research on Internet-mediated problematic behaviours has focused on either over-indulgence/addiction from overly relying on the Internet or showing various delinquent behaviour on the Internet.

First, regarding Internet addition, there is research on the risk factors and protective factors for such addiction. Kang and Son (2007) conducted a meta-analysis of previous research on Internet addiction and classified numerous factors into six main factors (self-related, emotion, family, peer, school, and Internet characteristics) in order to compare the effect size of each factor; the results showed the self-related factor and the peer factor as having the biggest effect. Self-related factors include self-esteem, self-control, and self-efficacy. The studies mainly discuss such factors and their relation to Internet addiction. Psychological factors were studied as the cause or the effect of Internet addiction. Whether such psychological factors are the cause or the effect of Internet addiction can be confirmed through longitudinal studies. For example, Park (2013) assumed self-esteem as the cause of Internet addiction and examined its influence. The results were that self-esteem level as a psychological factor, rather than other social-environmental factors or family-environmental factors, works as the main factor in developing Internet addiction. On the other hand, Park (2009) examined the effect of Internet addiction on middle school students' self-esteem, discovering that with more serious levels of Internet addiction, the longer the student had been using the Internet, the lower their self-esteem becomes.

Internet-mediated delinquency is often studied under the term of 'cyber delinquency'; factors affecting cyber delinquency can be described using social bonding theory, self-control theory, and delinquency opportunity theory. Social bonding theory sees that delinquency increases when one feels less bonded to surrounding people (Hirschi, 1969). Hirschi argues that the fear of weakening or breaking relationships with other members such as friends and parents due to one's own delinquency often controls the impulse to perpetrate any crime. Meanwhile, self-control theory argues that people perpetrate delinquency when they lose self-control momentarily in response to a temptation (Gottfredson and Hirschi, 1990). Bae (2016) carried out a six-year longitudinal survey of 3,449 students in 2nd grade at middle school; in his study, self-control was found to be a significant predictor for cyber delinquency. It showed a bigger predictor effect than strain factors (e.g., academic stress, conflicts with parents or friends) and social bonding factors (e.g., attachment-parents, supervision-parents, relationship with teachers). According to delinquency opportunity theory, even though one has high motivation or a tendency for delinquency, it is difficult to perpetrate any delinquency if there are no actual opportunities. Therefore, this theory postulates that the exposure to delinquency opportunity leads to the actual occurrence. For example, students who spend a longer time on the Internet are exposed to more cyber delinquency opportunities than others. Research supports the idea that the longer one uses the Internet, the more frequent cyber delinquency occurs (Bae, 2016; Lee, 2009).

In addition, numerous studies have explored various factors affecting cyber delinquency. The lack of ethics required in cyberspace was found to aggravate cyber delinquency (Cha, 2012). Personal psychological factors such as depression and aggression have also been found to have an effect (Kim, 2013). Lee and Choi (2018) also analysed the relationship between Internet-mediated problematic behaviours (over-reliance on cell phones and cyber delinquency) and emotion-behaviour problems, finding that the more serious someone's emotion-behaviour issues are, the more likely they are to be reliant on cell phones and the more serious cyber delinquency appears. According to Seo (2009), who analysed personal and environmental protective factors affecting such Internet-mediated problems, support from friends showed the most significant effect among all factors; in addition, students with such problems were more likely to have a low parent-supervision level and low family cohesiveness.

Japanese research on traditional/cyberbullying and Internet-mediated problems

Japanese research on school bullying

The recent trends in school bullying and violence in South Korea, introduced in Chapter 1, show a steady decrease after the implementation of the Comprehensive School Violence Eradication Plan in 2012. The situation in Japan is somewhat different from South Korea. The Bullying Prevention Promotion Act was implemented in 2013 but there has been steady increase in the number of recognised *ijime* cases. This is partly due to the difference in the definition of bullying in each country and partly due to differences in counting measurements.

Japanese statistics on *ijime* in schools have been affected by changes in measurement implemented by the government in 1994, 2006, and 2013. Such alterations and other minor changes are following media-focused incidents of '*ijime*-suicide'. Following the implementation of the Bullying Prevention Promotion Act in 2013, teachers are expected to count every glimpse of *ijime*. This explains why the numbers have increased sharply since then. However, when we focused on cyberbullying ('Being slandered or insulted through computers or cell phones etc.') among all the counts of *ijime* in 2018, counts of cyberbullying are 1% in elementary schools, 8% in junior-high schools, and 19% in high schools. These proportions are mostly the same as those from the previous year (2017).

Among the various topics of psychological research on *ijime*, we will focus on those that relate to three concerns: the help-seeking of victims and maintaining their anonymity, stopping the escalation of *ijime*, and the worst cases and long-term influence of *ijime*. This research is considered important for constructing and evaluating *ijime*-prevention/intervention practises.

To prevent victimization effectively, it is important to intervene not only at the school and classroom levels, but also at the individual level (Smith, Ananiadou, and Cowie, 2003). Views on victims' coping strategies have been compared between Eastern and Western countries (e.g. Kanetsuna and Smith, 2002); however, the coping strategies children use against *ijime* have been relatively unexamined. While there are many strategies that children use against bullying, one strategy is to tell others about acts of bullying and to seek help from an appropriate person (Smith and Shu, 2000). In school settings, teachers and friends are the most common helping resources (Mizuno and Ishikuma, 2004). However, some children fear that telling a teacher will result in even worse bullying (Fekkes, Pijpers, and Verloove-Vanhorick, 2005). Japanese children are more likely to seek help from their friends than from teachers or counsellors (Yamaguchi, Mizuno, and Ishikuma, 2004). Therefore, the establishment of a peer-support system (discussed later) appears to be one method for dealing with problems of *ijime*.

Studies in Western societies show that victims do not find it difficult to seek help from friends (Oliver and Candappa, 2007). However, among Japanese children, Nagai (2009) argues that children who report severe peer victimization are less likely to seek help from their friends. A scale of help-seeking behaviours was developed by Tamura and Ishikuma (2001). This scale assesses two dimensions of help-seeking expectations. One dimension is the view on how responsible the helper is expected to be when seeking help; the other dimension is feeling fear and concerns over the accessibility of help-seeking. In examining the relationship between victimization and expectations of receiving help from their friends, Mizuno, Yanagida, and Toda (2018) found that early teenage Japanese boys who were victimized may expect their friends' help (responsibility expectations), but their accessibility expectations may be rather pessimistic. Girls, however, did not show such results. Such tendencies suggest that the Q&A handout method (discussed below) would be effective, as children can report their suffering anonymously.

Kanetsuna, Smith, and Morita (2006) also suggested that because of the difficulty in finding external help as well as the fear that the ongoing *ijime* will get worse, targeted victims may be much more reluctant to seek help. Some media reports have criticised teachers for not being able to detect *ijime*, but we should keep in mind how difficult it is to do so if neither the perpetrators nor the victims report it.

As for stopping the escalation of *ijime*, Morita and colleagues (2001) reported the results of cross-national research that found that fewer young teenagers in Japan answered that they would try to stop others bullying than in the Netherlands and Britain. If Japanese children seem less willing to intervene in an *ijime* situation, is this a Japanese tendency? Perhaps we should consider the group process in Japanese schools when we think about *ijime* and its interventions.

In a school class where students are behaving aggressively, imbalances of power may emerge that can give rise to *ijime*. However, without factors maintaining these power imbalances and aggression, there should be no escalation of violence. This should also hold true for *ijime* in Japan, and researchers have investigated several factors that might affect escalation. Here, studies on justifications of aggressive behaviour, group processes, victims' attempts to cope with it, and other factors are summarised.

Justification of our behaviours is necessary in order to avoid self-punishment when we commit or continue prohibited behaviours. Bandura (1986) theorised this process as a dysfunctional mechanism of the self-regulation process, and later as a form of moral disengagement (e.g. Osofsky, Bandura, and Zimbardo, 2005). With respect to *ijime*, based on questionnaire research on junior-high school students, Inoue, Toda, and Nakamatsu (1986) elicited three reasoning factors used to justify bullying: sanctions, exclusion of minorities, and enjoyment. Using the same items, Onishi, Kurokawa, and Yoshida (2009) found two factors, where heterogeneity exclusion and enjoyment combined as one factor. Hara (2002) also looked at justifications for bullying among Japanese 12–14-year-old school children. Children with different types of involvement in bullying showed different justification strategies. In particular, bullies were more likely to blame the victims than were children assuming other roles.

Among the mechanisms of moral disengagement, 'diffusion of responsibility' brings collective harm without ascribing responsibility to a single person. If the number of perpetrators grows, a process of 'diffusion of responsibility' sets in and the violence may escalate. Recently, 'collective moral disengagement' has been a new focus of investigation (Gini, Pozzoli, and Bussey, 2014), and such a viewpoint should also be worth examining in the Japanese situation.

The increase in the number of perpetrators could be explained mainly by conformity. Some studies have looked in detail at the process of conformity in *ijime* episodes. Toda, Strohmeier, and Spiel (2008) showed a contingency between group size and frequency of victimization, in Japan and in Austria. When the aggression was not frequent, in half of the cases the number of perpetrators was one or two; on the other hand, when the aggression was frequent, in half of the cases in Austria and 80% of the cases in Japan, the perpetrators were a group. Kubota (2004) also showed that the number of assistants to the bullying and the kinds of bullying affect the duration of bullying.

Though justification by perpetrators and the group nature of bullying may escalate, victims do not just passively watch the unfolding of a tragedy. They try to change, but often in vain. Also, certain important factors steer the process in a particular direction. Honma (2003) tried to clarify the characteristics and factors relevant to the cessation of *ijime*, suggesting that intervention with students belonging to 'bullying-maintaining groups' should involve not only individual bullies, but also the bullying groups and other classroom members.

When such a group process is ongoing, intervention by just one hero/heroine would not ordinarily be effective, and furthermore, it could be dangerous by provoking perpetrators' anger and directing it against the intervener as the next target of *ijime*.

The worst cases of *ijime* in Japan so far are the numerous *ijime* suicides; some revenge murders of perpetrators by victims; and a few cases of the murder of victims by perpetrators. Mayama (2002) argued that '*ijime* suicide' (or suicide caused by bullying) was 'one of the most serious problems in Japanese primary and secondary schools since the late 1970s'. Though there have been many revenge rampage shootings by ex-victims of bullying in the U.S. (Larkin, 2013), at the time of writing there have been no cases of rampage shooting in Japanese schools (although there have been incidents with knives). However, there is no guarantee or reason for saying that such rampage shootings will never happen in Japan. Supporting and taking care of victims is also necessary to help prevent a very few but terrible cases of ex-victims fighting back against perpetrators, teachers, or schools.

Ishibashi and colleagues (1999) clarified the lasting effects of past victimization experiences (being bullied by peers) and their relationship to college students' tendencies to fear others. The long-lasting effects included suffering from various physical, behavioural, social, and psychological symptoms. However, those students who regarded themselves as having become more patient from having been bullied did not have a stronger tendency to fear others. Also, Miyake (2004) suggested a relationship between pre-adolescent bullying experiences and college students' attachment relationships. Their results suggest that experiences of being bullied can have lasting effects which continue after graduation from high school.

Mishima (2008) also investigated the long-term influence of bullying inflicted by intimate friends during the upper elementary school grades (5th and 6th grades). Among high school students, those who reported having been victimized in upper elementary school tended to show subsequent school maladjustment in high school, as well as feeling more anxiety towards interpersonal relationships than other students.

Some studies have focused on the buffering effects of recuperation. Kameda and Sagara (2011) held a semi-structured interview with young adults to examine the factors that enhanced the sense of self-growth among ex-victims. They found that a supportive relationship may help victims recuperate. In addition to support from others, the victim's own initiative in coping with the negative experience appeared to be important in attaining a feeling of self-growth.

As for the personal factors that buffer the negative effects of victimization, Araki (2005) investigated whether resilience contributes to victims' adjustment in young adulthood. Participants in the questionnaire research were Japanese young adults with a mean age of about 20 years. Those who had been peer-victimized during childhood had greater distress and anxiety than those who had not, although no difference was found in the levels of exposure to current interpersonal stressful events. The distress and anxiety were stronger for men than women, and the starting age of victimization made no difference to the severity of the problems. Both problem-focused and support-seeking coping as protective factors had a compensatory effect on the long-term negative outcomes of victimization by peers during childhood.

Japanese research on cyberbullying

Following the rapid spread of Internet-connected mobile devices among children and adolescents in the late 1990s to early 2000s, there has been wide media coverage of children and adolescents' involvement in various online risk behaviours. These include excessive use and the tendency to become dependent on mobile devices and on various online activities, inappropriate posting to various Social Networking Services (SNS), using and exchanging abusive language, and accessing sexual and violent materials.

According to the latest national survey on Internet use among young people in 2018, about 86% (41%) of primary, 95% (66%) of junior-high, and 99% (95%) of high school students in Japan use some kind of Internet-connected devices regularly (numbers in brackets are those who use some kind of smartphones), and among these, about 85% of primary, 95% of junior-high, and 99% of high school students reported using the Internet (Cabinet Office, 2019). In terms of what they are using the Internet for, 'playing online games' is the most frequent response (76%) among primary school children, followed by 'watching videos' (62%), 'communication (incl. email, messenger services, and SNS)' (33%), and 'searching and browsing particular information' (33%). Among junior-high school students, 'communication' comes first (76%), followed by 'watching videos' (75%), 'playing online games' (67%), 'listening to music' (63%), and 'searching and browsing' (54%). Similarly, among high school students, 'communication' again comes first (90%), followed by 'watching videos' (85%), 'listening to music' (79%), 'playing online games' (72%), and 'searching and browsing' (68%) (Japanese Cabinet Office, 2019).

Regarding the prevalence of cyberbullying, the Japanese Ministry of Education, Culture, Sports, Science and Technology (MEXT) reported that about 1% (primary), 8% (junior-high) or 18% (high school) of all bullying victims were victimized through the Internet in some way in fiscal year 2017, and the figures has remained almost flat for the past five years (MEXT, 2018). These figures may give the impression that cyberbullying in Japan is not so serious, particularly among primary and junior-high school students. However, this is not necessarily true given the following points (among others). First, although the levels of cyberbullying as a percentage of the total number of recognised bullying incidents at school is certainly flat, the actual number of recognised cyberbullying cases is increasing every year with the increase in the total number of recognised bullying cases. Second and more importantly, as Smith (2012) stressed, there are a number of distinctive features of cyberbullying that are different from traditional bullying, and which make it even more difficult to prevent or intervene in. The invisibility or anonymity of the perpetrators is one such feature. We will discuss this in detail later in this chapter, but because of this particular characteristic, cyberbullying is probably more complicated and more difficult for us to intervene in than traditional bullying. The concept of repetition, which is often considered one of the major conditions of traditional bullying, is another distinctive feature of cyberbullying that can be more difficult to operationalise. In cyberspace, even if the perpetration is only a single act, it can be seen, commented on, distorted, exaggerated, and forwarded by many others, and this clearly constitutes a concept of repetition (Smith, 2012). Based on these unique characteristics of the Internet, Smith warns that we should not judge the seriousness of cyberbullying only by the simple number of reported cases of perpetration and victimization as we often do for traditional bullying.

Furthermore, cyberbullying is merely a part of Internet-mediated problems among children. The national survey mentioned above revealed that about 15% of students reported having received junk emails and messages, and 13% of them reported experiencing lack of sleep during the night and lack of concentration during the day because of their excessive use of the Internet. About 3% reported having received nasty comments from unknown people or to have posted nasty comments about others (Japanese Cabinet Office, 2019). In recent years, it has been reported that junior-high school and high school students have been sent documents from the prosecutor on suspicion of violating the Child Prostitution and Pornography Prohibition Act by disseminating videos of naked classmates using their smartphones (Sankei News Paper, 2018). The National Police Agency (NPA) reported that the number of child pornography cases in fiscal 2017 was the highest in any one year, and that 40% of the victimized children had taken naked images and uploaded them on the Internet themselves (NPA, 2018).

The surveys introduced above are conducted by the Government and the NPA at the national level. Turning to academic research, some early studies focus on the effect of using cell phones and the Internet on interpersonal relationships among youth. For example, Kohara (2004) reported that students have become reluctant to form new friendships because they are able to communicate with existing friends at any time they want, even when they are away from each other. Around 2010, when the spread of mobile devices had increased further, more research was conducted on the repercussions of students' excessive use and their tendency to depend on such devices. Okamoto and colleagues (2014) examined the general usage of the Internet among university students, and reported that those with higher levels of dependency on the Internet showed significantly higher levels of various mental health problems including depression, anxiety, loneliness, and poor interpersonal relationships. In terms of the studies on cyberbullying and other online deviant behaviours, the effects of anonymity on the Internet has been verified. The effect and impact of anonymity on the Internet is discussed in detail in Chapter 8. Although the statistical surveys at the national level have continued in Japan, academic research still seems to be insufficient compared to South Korea. It will be necessary to increase this research, including comparative studies between Japan and South Korea.

The results of the National survey and the reports from the NPA discussed above suggest that many children in Japan seem familiar with various mobile devices and regularly use them for accessing the Internet. But at the same time, it appears that they are not necessarily using the Internet in appropriate manner. Therefore, it seems to be a good idea to use online games and apps to learn about various online risks including cyberbullying, and to acquire proper knowledge and skills of online literacy and morality to prevent involvement in such risky situations on the Internet.

Japanese research on the other Internet-mediated problems

Moving on to Japanese research on Internet addiction, Higuchi (2017) warns that the activity of the frontal cortex is refrained when one is addicted to the Internet. This may cause the difficulty of suppressing impulsiveness. The weaker the function of the frontal lobe is, the more difficult it is for the person to control their impulses for games and so on. In addition, Higuchi (2018) reports that in the striatum in the basal ganglia among people with Internet addition, there appeared a lack of reaction of the 'reward system'. This may suggest that in the brains of people who depend on the Internet and games, the number of receptors for the neurotransmitter dopamine related to pleasure has decreased, making it difficult to feel pleasure.

In addition to such bio-chemical mechanisms, Higuchi (2017) proposes a typology of three categories of people who are addicted to the Internet. The first group is characterised as people who have liked various games including betting games since their childhood, and who have fairly good school performance. The second group includes people who are not good at building/maintaining good relations with others. They may have experienced interpersonal troubles, which triggered their withdrawal, and they can only keep in contact with the others on the Internet.

The last group is people with a tendency of ADHD (Attention Deficit Hyperactivity Disorder), ASD (Autism Spectrum Disorder), or social anxiety disorder. Children with ADHD may just continue to use the Internet without any definite purpose. Children with ASD may just feel safe on the Internet because of their not being able to adjust themselves to ambiguous situations. Children with social anxiety disorder may also only feel safe in their own world on the Internet, rather than in face-to-face situations, which causes them too much tension.

Such tendencies may be somewhat related to their family situation. Children watch how their family members use the Internet and follow in a similar way (Endoh, 2015). Kiyokawa and Utsumi (2014) point out that 'Sumaho-ikuji', which means over-usage of smartphones and tablets in order to soothe infants, may obstruct attachment and prepare their addiction to the Internet. In schools, chats in SNS and games with friends may last until midnight sometimes, leading to a lack of sleep and disruption of daily life. Also, in using SNS, sometimes replying slowly is regarded as 'ignoring', and because of the fear of being bullied following such a misunderstanding, some children do not feel able to let go of their cell phone at any time. This kind of case should be understood as Internet addiction caused by relationship dependency and peer pressure. In addition, when many classmates are using the Internet, it may be difficult for individuals to realise they are using the Internet excessively (Endoh, 2013). Schools are now actively incorporating lessons and learning using computers and tablets, making it difficult for schools themselves to limit excessive use of the Internet.

Such factors may be multi-dimensionally affecting the Internet addiction of Japanese children. That's why our countermeasures to cope with Internet addiction should also be constructed from multiple aspects. School teachers, family members, and other professionals should collaborate more to lead to the better use of the Internet by children.

Turning to Japanese research on other Internet-mediated problems, Usui (2008) has discussed and categorised various problems around Internet communication in his review. In addition to aggression and addiction, he lists the problems of 'inappropriate acquaintance' and 'suicide induction' via the Internet. Chiba, Fujimura, and Takahashi (2009) also focused on the problems such as 'dating sites', 'suicide induction sites', 'child-pornography distribution', and 'threatening to commit a crime' on the Internet together with cyberbullying. Concerning these problems, they summarised the background of the problems and governmental/non-governmental countermeasures. Though it is difficult to count the number of victims/perpetrators by age group and by such categorisations, it seems that the proportion of victimized children would be much higher than the proportion of perpetrating children. This is particularly the case for sexual crimes, where children are mostly victims of adult perpetrators. As these are criminal cases, it is the police rather than schools who are responsible for investigating and responding to such cases and there are very few studies concerning this topic.

After their research in Tokyo (Chiba and Takahashi, 2010), Chiba and colleagues (2013) reported the results of a ten-country comparison (Japan, China, South Korea, Singapore, UK, Germany, France, Finland, USA, and Chile) by randomised telephone interviews with 330 persons (15–69 years old) in each country (3,300 in total) concerning their views on harmful information on the Internet. The research was conducted in 2010, and at that stage the proportions of using filtering services in Japan was 38.5%. Among other countries, some were higher (UK 78.1%, China 61.7%, USA 58.8%, Singapore 56.7%, Germany 51.4%), some were similar (France 39.6%, Finland 38.6%, South Korea 37.2%), while Chile was lower (12.8%) at that stage. In Japan only, the use of filtering services was higher among participants who have children. In Japan, China, South Korea, and Germany, the proportions of feeling anxiety about children viewing harmful information (information about pornography and drugs) on the Internet was around 80% and higher than in other countries.

Future research perspectives of South Korea and Japan

Located nearby and sharing similar cultural backgrounds in comparison to Western countries, Japan and South Korea have somewhat similar research on bullying, cyberbullying, and the other Internet-mediated problems, however there are also some differences. The bullying problem, represented by *wang-ta* in Korea and *ijime* in Japan, is taking on a new phase as traditional bullying has been turning into cyberbullying. Since anonymity affects participants' behaviours in cyberbullying much more than in traditional bullying, cyberbullying can show unique characteristics in South Korea and Japan compared to Western countries. This is because in Eastern cultures compared to the West, there seems to be a high sensitivity to how others look at you, namely social perspective. As we have tried in this book, efforts to analyse cyberbullying from a cultural perspective will be even more necessary in the future.

Regarding bullying research, it seems that there is not much difference between the two countries. This may be mostly due to the fact that both countries are working closely with international researchers. However, based on the authors' personal experiences, Japanese researchers work in collaboration with European and Australian researchers, while keeping our own research interests on the specific traits of *ijime*. In contrast, Korean research trends are much more connected to North American trends, and are growing rapidly more focused on cyberbullying. Such tendencies may mostly depend on where researchers from each country stayed, studied, and collaborated. Research trends on traditional bullying are very much rooted in Scandinavian countries, and famous countermeasures were invented there. However, from the mid-2000s, cyberbullying research has been growing rapidly in North America. That's why future research collaboration between South Korea and Japan will help in merging big research trends worldwide. In addition, future research in South Korea and Japan is expected to focus on specific aspects of the problems and countermeasures in Eastern countries and on more detailed varieties in both countries.

As for Internet addiction, South Korea and Japan seem to share similar views of its seriousness and have a similar level of concern in society. In both countries, studies on factors contributing to Internet addiction are increasing. However, both countries are still struggling to find effective measures to prevent and cope with the problem. In comparison to the research and practices to reduce traditional/cyberbullying, efforts and trials are scarce in the area of the Internet addiction. We cannot find a comparable prevalence study using the same scales for both countries. One of the reasons is the development and use of various kinds of scales to measure Internet addiction. We need a good scale which has fairly well-established psychometrics in order to compare the prevalence and/or characteristics of Internet addiction among various Asian countries. However, researchers and practitioners who are tackling Internet addiction problems seem to be fully occupied in handling problems in their own countries.

However, regarding other Internet-mediated problems, the picture is much more complex and confused than the way we see cyberbullying and Internet addiction. It is very difficult to develop an invariant scale that can be applied to such diverse and complex phenomenon worldwide. Before we can develop such a scale, we would need to categorise the other Internet-mediated problems, which include sexual problems, financial problems, suicidal induction, and so on. New problems are also emerging and those make the recent categorisation framework less effective. Also, we have to note the fact that such problems are not just happening inside schools or among mostly children and teachers/parents. Outsiders with harmful and selfish motivations are contacting children via the Internet. The problems are beyond school psychology or education. Cyberbullying is being studied in a wide variety of fields, including education, psychology, ICT (Information, Communications and Technology), criminology, and so on. Each field studies a specific area of cyberbullying based on different academic disciplines. For example, education emphasises educational intervention to reduce cyberbullying, while psychology emphasises psychological characteristics that affect cyberbullying, and ICT emphasises the technological aspects of newly changing cyberbullying. Therefore, we need wider collaboration with a variety of social science disciplines in order to gain a better understanding and to provide more effective interventions.

So far, many studies on cyberbullying have focused on risk factors (e.g., aggression, moral dislocation, etc.) that affect bullying and on negative consequences of bullying (e.g., anxiety, depression, suicide, etc.). An approach that reduces cyberbullying by diminishing risk factors is effective, but at the same time an approach is being sought to reduce cyberbullying by increasing protective factors that inhibit cyberbullying. With the recent expansion of positive psychology, the importance of positive psychological variables (e.g. resilience) to effectively control cyberbullying is emphasised (Hinduja and Patchin, 2017; Papatraianou, Levine, and West, 2014). Therefore, future research looks forward to the studies investigating positive variables that effectively inhibit cyberbullying and make cyberspace safer. The ultimate goal of education and psychology is not to eliminate problems, but to further strengthen capabilities in dealing with problems and create nurturing environments despite problems.

References

Araki, T. (2005). Resilience in a personal history of peer victimization: What factors contribute to victims' adjustment in young adulthood? *Japanese Journal of Personality*, *14*, 54–68. doi:10.2132/personality.14.54

Bae, S. M. (2016). The influence of strain factors, social bonding, self-control, amount of internet use, offline delinquency on adolescent cyber delinquency- analysis for longitudinal data during four years by hierarchical linear modeling. *Korean Journal of Counseling*, *17*(6), 381–394. doi:10.15703/kjc.17.6.201612.381

Bandura, A. (1986). *Social Foundations of Thought and Action: A Social Cognitive Theory*. Englewood Cliffs, NJ: Prentice-Hall.

Bronfenbrenner, U. (1979). *The Ecology of Human Development: Experiments by Nature and Design*. Cambridge, MA: Harvard University Press.

Bronfenbrenner, U. (1994). Ecological models of human development. *Readings on the Development of Children*, *2*(1), 37–43.

Cabinet Office (2019). *Survey on Environment of the Internet Usage for Adolescents*. Tokyo: Cabinet Office, Government of Japan.

Cha, E. J. (2012). A study on factors influencing middle school students' cyber delinquency. *Journal of Adolescent Welfare*, *14*(3), 1–27.

Chiba, N., Fujimura, A., and Takahashi, K. (2009). Latest trends and studies of some problems that caused by illegal and harmful information on the Internet. *IPSJ SIG Technical Reports*, *44*, 115–120.

Chiba, N. and Takahashi, K. (2010). A study of countermeasures against harmful information on the internet from users' point of view. *IPSJ Journal*, *51*, 1702–1710.

Chiba, N., Yamamoto, T., Seki, Y., Takahashi, K., Ogasahara, M., Sekiya, N., Nakamura, I., and Hashimoto, Y. (2013). International comparative study of users' awareness to harmful information on the internet. *IPSJ Journal*, *54*, 1619–1631.

Cho, Y. J. (2006). *Moderating variables on the transition to bullies of witnesses or victims of bullying (wang-ta in Korean)* (Unpublished doctoral thesis). Sookmyung Women's University, Seoul, South Korea.

Choi, M. K. (2006). The relations of children's peer victimization, self-esteem, and loneliness. *Korean Journal of Child Studies*, *27*(4), 133–145.

Chun, D. I., Wie, S. K., Choi, J. B., and Oh, B. Y. (2008). Characteristics of cyber delinquency and influence factors. *Journal of Social Welfare Review*, *13*, 149–170.

Do, G. B. (2008). The interaction effects between factors in ecology system and aggression affecting school violence. *Journal of Adolescent Welfare, 10*, 73–92.
Do, G. B. and Lee, Y. H. (2009). A study on the influence of peer misdeed and teacher's corporal punishment upon school violence: Focused on moderating effect of domestic violence. *Journal of Social Welfare Development, 15*(3), 225–245.
Endoh, M. (2013). *For Avoiding the Internet and Smartphone Addiction*. Tokyo: Seibundo-Shinkosha.
Endoh, M. (2015). *The Internet Addiction Among Children: Prevention and Countermeasures from Elementary School Age*. Kyoto: Kamogawa Shuppan.
Fanti, K. A., Demetriou, A. G., and Hawa, V. V. (2012). A longitudinal study of cyberbullying: Examining risk and protective factors. *European Journal of Developmental Psychology, 9*(2), 168–181. doi:10.1080/17405629.2011.643169
Fekkes, M., Pijpers, F. I. M., and Verloove-Vanhorick, S. P. (2005). Bullying: Who does what, when and where? Involvement of children, teachers and parents in bullying behavior. *Health Education Research: Theory & Practice, 20*(1), 81–91. doi:10.1093/her/cyg100
Ghim, H. R. (2012). Differences of cognitive and affective empathy by participant roles in bullying among 5th and 6th grade Korean children. *The Korean Journal of Developmental Psychology, 26*(4), 1–20.
Gini, G., Pozzoli, T., and Bussey, K. (2014). Collective moral disengagement: Initial validation of a scale for adolescents. *European Journal of Developmental Psychology, 11*, 386–395. doi:10.1080/17405629.2013.851024
Gottfredson, M. R. and Hirschi, T. (1990). *A General Theory of Crime*. Stanford, CA: Stanford University Press.
Hara, H. (2002). Justifications for bullying among Japanese schoolchildren. *Asian Journal of Social Psychology, 5*, 197–204. doi:10.1111/1467-839X.00104
Higuchi, S. (2017). *How to Protect Children from 'the Internet Addiction' that Erodes Mental and Physical Health*. Kyoto: Minerva Shobo.
Higuchi, S. (2018). *The Internet and Game Addiction*. Tokyo: Kodansha.
Hinduja, S. and Patchin, J. W. (2017). Cultivating youth resilience to prevent bullying and cyberbullying victimization. *Child Abuse and Neglect, 73*, 51–62. doi:10.1016/j.chiabu.2017.09.010
Hirschi, T. (1969). *A Control Theory of Delinquency*. Criminology Theory: Selected Classic Readings, *1969*, 289–305.
Hong, S. H. (2016). The effect of father attachment as perceived by adolescents on exerted experience of school violence: Focused on the mediating effect of interpersonal relationship. *Journal of Welfare for the Correction, 45*, 153–182.
Hong, Y. S. and Kim, D. K. (2011). Structural relation of juvenile stress, self-esteem, self-control and cyber delinquency: Testing a sex difference. *Korean Journal of Youth Studies, 18*(1), 127–148.
Honma, T. (2003). Cessation of bullying and intervention with bullies: Junior high school students. *Japanese Journal of Educational Psychology, 51*, 390–400. doi:10.5926/jjep1953.51.4_390
Inoue, K., Toda, Y., and Nakamatsu, M. (1986). Roles in bullying situation. *Bulletin of the Faculty of Education, University of Tokyo, 26*, 89–106.
Ishibashi, S., Wakabayashi, S., Naito, T., and Shikano, T. (1999). An investigation of the lasting effects of peer victimization in college students: Relationship to anthropophagic tendencies. *Bulletin of Christian Culture Studies, Kinjo Gakuin University, 3*, 11–19.

Japanese Ministry of Education, Culture, Sports, Science and Technology (MEXT) (2018). *Annual Fact-finding Survey on Problematic Behavior in School.* Tokyo: MEXT, Government of Japan.

Jue, J. and Kwon, S. M. (2001). Types of problematic behaviors in internet usage and their classification: Based upon domestic cases. *Psychological Science*, *10*(1), 93–115.

Jun, S. H. and Lee, S. S. (2010). Exploring explanatory factors for youth's cyber-bullying by cell phone. *Korean Journal of Youth Studies*, *17*(11), 159–181.

Kameda, H. and Sagara, J. (2011). Effect of past bullied experiences and factors that help develop feelings of self-growth: Examination of the development process involving past bullied experiences and the current awareness of self-growth. *Japanese Journal of Counseling Science*, *44*, 277–287. doi:10.11544/cou.44.4_277

Kanetsuna, T. and Smith, P. K. (2002). Pupil insights into bullying, and coping with bullying: A binational study in Japan and England. *Journal of School Violence*, *1*, 5–29. doi:10.1300/J202v01n03_02

Kanetsuna, T., Smith, P. K., and Morita, Y. (2006). Coping with bullying at school: Children's recommended strategies and attitudes to school-based interventions in England and Japan. *Aggressive Behavior*, *32*, 570–580. doi:10.1002/ab.20156

Kang, H. Y. and Son, C. N. (2007). A meta-analysis on the variables related Internet and game addiction. *The Korean Journal of Health Psychology*, *12*(4), 733–744. doi:10.17315/kjhp.2007.12.4.004

Kang, S. Y. (2012). A grounded theory based approach on school violence. *Korean Criminal Psychology Review*, *8*(2), 5–28.

Kim, E. K. (2012). *A study on the predictors of youth's cyber bullying* (Unpublished doctoral thesis). Myongji University, Seoul, South Korea.

Kim, E. Y. (2014). An investigation of factors influencing on adolescents' bullying behaviors: An examination of the impact of bullying victimization and exposure to inter-parental violence. *Journal of Korean Public Police and Security Studies*, *11*(1), 1–22. doi:10.25023/kapsa.11.1.201405.1

Kim, H. H. (2002). The relation between bullying-victimization and adolescents' self-esteem: The implication of peer support. *Family and Environment Research*, *40*(9), 47–61.

Kim, J. H. (2013). Influence of depression and aggression of adolescents on cyber and real-world delinquency mediated by types of internet use. *Journal of School Social Work*, *24*, 31–59.

Kim, J. S. and Moon, H. J. (2016). The effects of academic stress, school atmosphere, family communication on school violence in adolescence: Mediating effects of fear of school violence. *Journal of the Korea Institute of Youth Facility and Environment*, *14*(2), 95–108.

Kim, J-Y., Chung, Y-K., and Lee, J-S. (2008). The contribution of adolescents' exposure to marital violence on school violence: Moderating effect of supportive social networks. *Journal of Korean Youth Research*, *15*, 89–115.

Kim, K. E. (2012). Mediating effect of aggression on the relationship between family-violence experience and cyber violence in youth. *Journal of Future Oriented Youth Society*, *9*(4), 51–73.

Kim, K. E. and Choi, E. H. (2012). A study on the effect of school violence victimization on adolescents' cyber violence: Focus on mediating effect of aggression. *Journal of Adolescent Welfare*, *14*(3), 259–283.

Kim, K. E. and Choi, E. H. (2017). The relationship between school-violence victimization and cyber-violence behavior in youth: The mediating effect of cyber-violence victimization. *Journal of School Social Work, 38*, 75–97. dx.doi: 10.20993/jSSW.38.4

Kim, M. J. (2002). *Construction of a predictive model of adolescents' school violent behavior* (Unpublished doctoral thesis). GwangJu, South Korea: Chonnam National University.

Kim, M. Y. (2007). The effects of the school-system on middle school students' bullying. *Studies on Korean Youth, 18*(2), 287–314.

Kim, S. C. and Ko, J. H. (2014). The relationships between school violence and use of conflict resolution strategies: Roles of family and class cohesion. *Journal of Educational Theory and Practice, 24*, 25–43.

Kim, S-H. (2006). The developmental and contextual analysis on school violence. *The Korean Journal of Educational Psychology, 20*, 1027–1042.

Kim, W. Y. and Kim, K. S. (2018). A meta-analysis on the triggering variables related to school violence behaviors in Korea. *Journal of Secondary Education Research, 66*(3), 783–814. doi:10.25152/ser.2018.66.3.783

Kiyokawa, T. and Utsumi, H. (2014). *Children Damaged by 'Addiction to the Media'*. Tokyo: Juniors' Visual Journal.

Kohara, K. (2004). The influence of the diffusion of mobile phones to the relationships of university students. *Socio-Cultural Studies of Education, 10*, 1–17.

Kubota, M. (2004). Can the coping behaviors of bullied children provide effective alternatives to bullying? Attempts to modify the stigmatic labels given by gangs of bullies. *Journal of Educational Sociology, 74*, 249–268. doi:10.11151/eds1951.74.249

Kwon, H. Y. and Kim, H. M. (2009). The qualitative analysis on psycho-social factors of bullying adolescent at school violence. *The Korean Journal of East West Science, 12*(1), 1–12.

Larkin, R. W. (2013). Legitimated adolescent violence: Lessons from Columbine. In N. Böckler, T. Seeger, P. Sitzer, and W. Heitmeyer (eds.), *School Shootings: International Research, Case Studies, and Concepts for Prevention* (pp. 159–176). New York: Springer Science + Business Media.

Lee, C. J. and Kwak, K. J. (2000). Self-concept, social support according to bullying types. *The Korean Journal of Developmental Psychology, 13*(1), 65–80.

Lee, E. K. and Kim, B. S. (2012). The effect of the familial protective factor and the individual protective factor on the adjustment of adolescent peer-bullying victims. *Korean Journal of Counseling, 13*(2), 725–743. doi:10.15703/kjc.13.2.201204.725

Lee, H. and Kim, H. (2001). Social and psychological variables predicting elementary students' school bullying behaviors: On the bases of their gender and grade. *Korean Journal of Social and Personality Psychology, 15*(1), 117–138.

Lee, H. H. and Kim, H. W. (2000). The effect of violence-exposure on school bullying: On the bases of the interaction effects between violence-exposure and psychological variables. *The Korean Journal of Developmental Psychology, 13*(1), 95–113.

Lee, M. J. (2004). A study on the ecosystematic variables of bullying behavior among elementary school students. *Korean Journal of Clinical Social Work, 1*(1), 41–61.

Lee, S. S. (2005). The effects of anonymity on cyber flaming: Comparing its effect with social and individual factors. *Studies on Korean Youth, 16*(1), 77–108.

Lee, S. S. (2007). Testing a model of cyber-delinquency through motive, opportunity and control factors. *Informatization Policy, 14*(3), 3–15.

Lee, S. S. (2009). The effects of strain, low self-control, and internet time use on cyber delinquency: Testing three theories of delinquency. *Korean Criminology Review, 20*(1), 95–115.

Lee, S., Oh, I., and Lee, J. (2014). Psychosocial characteristics of bullies, victims, bully-victims among elementary school students. *Korean Journal of Youth Studies, 21*(5), 391–416.

Lee, Y. J. and Choi, M. S. (2018). Profiles of emotional and behavior problems as predictors of problematic internet use in adolescents. *Journal of Lerner-Centered Curriculum and Instruction, 18*(12), 497–521. doi:10.22251/jlcci.2018.18.12.497

Lee, S. Y. and Oh, I. (2012). School violence in South Korea: An overview of school violence and intervention efforts. In S. Jimerson, M. Furlong, A. Nickerson, and M. Mayer (eds.), *Handbook of School Violence and School Safety: International Research and Practice* (2nd ed.) (pp. 541–553). New York: Routledge.

Li, M. J. and Oh, I. S. (2017). Effect of elementary school student's domestic violence experience and aggression on school violence behavior according to gender: Moderated mediation effect of ego-resiliency. *The Journal of Educational Studies, 48*(3), 23–46. doi:10.15854/jes.2017.09.48.3.23

Mayama, H. (2002). Discourse analysis as conceptual study: Toward the dismantling of *ijime* suicide. *Journal of Educational Sociology, 70*, 145–163. doi:10.11151/eds1951.70.145

Mishima, K. (2008). Long-term influence of 'bullying' received from intimate friends during upper elementary school grades: Focusing on retrospect of high school students. *Japanese Journal of Experimental Social Psychology, 47*, 91–104. doi:10.2130/jjesp.47.91

Miyake, K. (2004). Adult attachment and victimization of bullying. *Journal of Kyushu University of Health and Welfare, 5*, 1–10. doi:10.15069/00000520

Mizuno, H. and Ishikuma, T. (2004). An overview of studies on social support for children: Some implications for research and practice in school psychology in Japan. *Japanese Journal of Counseling Science, 37*, 280–290. doi:10.5926/jjep1953.54.1_75

Mizuno, H., Yanagida, T., and Toda, Y. (2018). How help-seeking expectations are associated with relational and physical victimization among Japanese adolescents. *Psychology, 9*, 1412–1425. doi:10.4236/psych.2018.96086

Morita, Y., Soeda, H., Taki, M., Hoshino, K., Takemura, K., Matsu'ura, Y., Hata, M., Yonezato, S., Takekawa, I., and Soeda, K. (2001). *Cross-national Studies on Bullying*. Tokyo: Kaneko Shobo.

Nagai, S. (2009). Help-seeking intentions of elementary school students: Relationship with satisfaction with school life, experience of concerns and depression. *Japanese Journal of School Psychology, 9*, 17–24. doi:10.24583/jjspedit.9.1_17

National Police Agency (2018). *Current Status and Countermeasures of Children Affected by SNS in Fiscal 2017*. Tokyo: NPA.

Oh, I. (2010). Psychological factors influencing bystanders' behavioral reactions to bullying: A focus on empathy and aggression. *The Journal of Elementary Education, 23*(1), 45–63.

Okamoto, Y., Miyake, Y., Jinnin, R., Yashiki, H., Uchino, T., Isobe, N., and Yoshihara, M. (2014). The Internet use situation in university students: Association between tendency of dependence and mental condition. *Sogo Hoken Kagaku, 30*, 7–13. doi:10.15027/35440

Oliver, C. and Candappa, M. (2007). Bullying and the politics of 'telling'. *Oxford Review of Education, 33*, 71–86. doi:10.1080/03054980601094594

Onishi, A., Kurokawa, M., and Yoshida, T. (2009). Influences of students' teacher recognition on abuse. *Japanese Journal of Educational Psychology, 57*, 324–335. doi:10.5926/jjep.57.324

Osofsky, M. J., Bandura, A., and Zimbardo, P. G. (2005). The role of moral disengagement in the execution process. *Law and Human Behavior, 29*, 371–393. doi:10.1007/s10979-005-4930-1

Papatraianou, L. H., Levine, D., and West, D. (2014). Resilience in the face of cyberbullying: An ecological perspective on young people's experiences of online adversity. *Pastoral Care in Education, 32*(4), 264–283. doi:10.1080/02643944.2014.974661

Park, E. S. (2009). The effects of internet addictive tendency on the self-esteem and leisure activities of middle school students. *Journal of Counseling Psychology, 9*(1), 1–35. doi:10.5897/ijpc2016.0459

Park, J. H. (2006). Causes of school violence and the exploration of policy alternatives as its solution. *Correction Welfare Research, 5*, 215–239.

Park, J. Y. (2017). The relationships of adolescent academic stress, school violence and subjective happiness: Focusing on the mediating pathway of friend, family and teacher's support. *Journal of Social Science, 43*(2), 263–289. doi:10.15820/khjss.2017.43.2.011

Park, S. G. (2013). A study on the internet addiction affected by the level of self-esteem. *Journal of the Korea Society of Computer and Information, 18*(11), 153–158. dx.doi: 10.9708/jksci.2013.18.11.153

Sankei News Paper (2018). *Aichi Prefectural Police Department, 14 High School Students Sent Documents by Spreading Naked Videos of Friend Girl on LINE*. 2018.8.17. 19:17. Retrieved from www.sankei.com/west/news/180817/wst1808170085-n1.html

Seo, J. A. (2009). The effects of personal and environmental protective factors on internet problem behaviors of youth. *Korean Juvenile Protection Review, 12*, 125–160.

Seo, J. H. and Choi, Y. S. (2016). The influence of bullying victimization experience in adolescence on the male and female university students' social anxiety: The moderating effect of family resilience. *Korean Journal of Counseling, 17*(1), 327–343. doi:10.15703/kjc.17.1.201602.327

Shin, H, Y. (2015). Friend influence on aggressive and pro-social behaviors in elementary schools: Significance of peer network based school counseling. *The Journal of Korea Elementary Education, 26*(3), 219–235. doi:10.20972/kjee.26.3.201509.219

Shin, N. M. (2012). Empathy and bullying: How are they related in explaining the types of bullying participations among adolescents? *Journal of Adolescent Welfare, 14*(4), 25–45.

Shin, S. R. (2016). How does juvenile's witness of violence, watch of violence media affect traditional bullying and cyber bullying? *Journal of Welfare for the Correction, 44*, 139–158.

Smith, P. K. (2012). Cyberbullying challenges and opportunities for a research program: A response to Olweus (2012). *European Journal of Developmental Psychology, 9*(5), 553–558. doi:10.1080/17405629.2012.689821

Smith, P. K., Ananiadou, K., and Cowie, H. (2003). Interventions to reduce school bullying. *The Canadian Journal of Psychiatry, 48*(9), 591–599. doi:10.1177/070674370304800905

Smith, P. K. and Shu, S. (2000). What good schools can do about bullying: Findings from a survey in English schools after a decade of research and action. *Childhood, 7*, 193–212. doi:10.1177/0907568200007002005

Sung, D. K., Kim, D. H., Lee, Y. S., and Lim, S. Y. (2006). A study on the cyber-violence induction factors of teenagers: Focused on individual inclination, cyber violence damage experience, and moral consciousness. *Journal of Cyber Communication Academic Society, 19*, 79–129.

Tamura, S. and Ishikuma, T. (2001). Help-seeking preferences and burnout: Junior high school teachers in Japan. *Japanese Journal of Educational Psychology, 49*, 438–448. doi:10.5926/jjep1953.54.1_75

Toda, Y., Strohmeier, D., and Spiel, C. (2008). Process model of bullying. In T. Katoh and H. Taniguchi (eds.), *Darkside of Interpersonal Relationships* (pp. 117–131). Kyoto: Kitaohji-Shobo.

Usui, M. (2008). The review of the problems and possibilities on the Internet communication. *Graduate School of Niigata Seiryo University Journal of Clinical Psychology, 2*, 71–79.

Yamaguchi, T., Mizuno, H., and Ishikuma, T. (2004). Relationship between perceived problems and help-seeking preferences in junior high students. *Japanese Journal of Counseling Science, 34*, 241–249.

3 Level of Immersion in Media Experience (LIME) model

Akihiko Ieshima

This chapter presents a new idea of the LIME model, which locates an individual's level of immersion of media experience. The LIME model enables us to understand how children experience media. This chapter discusses the following three points: 1) the reason why the LIME model is necessary, 2) how the model was elicited, and 3) possibility of the model to be used in preventing bullying (including cyberbullying) and other Internet-mediated problems.

Necessity of the model for understanding

When children's positive/negative experiences through media are discussed, terms such as virtual/real, online/offline, and so on are usually used. However, virtual views and real views overlap already, and online experiences may vary due to ongoing developments in digital technologies. In Chapter 2, such overlapping was not mentioned so that each phenomenon and its related research could be understood separately. However, in the following chapters children's experiences should be understood in comparison to those of others. To explore their various experiences, I introduce a new model (Figure 3.1). After I depicted the model, other authors and the editors of this book discussed it, and I improved it in response. In the next paragraph, I introduce the model in detail before showing related models that in turn elicit a new model. Following those explanations, some implications in using the model are discussed. In the following chapters, I provide various cases to highlight the contours of the model.

Level of Immersion in Media Experience (LIME) model

In level 1 (Audience mode), people experience the media as an audience. The level of immersion is superficial and very shallow. The level of commitment is weak. The subjective behavior is a state of viewing or reading, and the experience type is indirect. The person is experiencing someone else's story from a third-party perspective. For example, watching TV is a way to empathize with the emotions of the characters and to feel the story indirectly. People sympathize with the emotions of the characters, but at the same time, the distance is maintained by looking at the characters objectively.

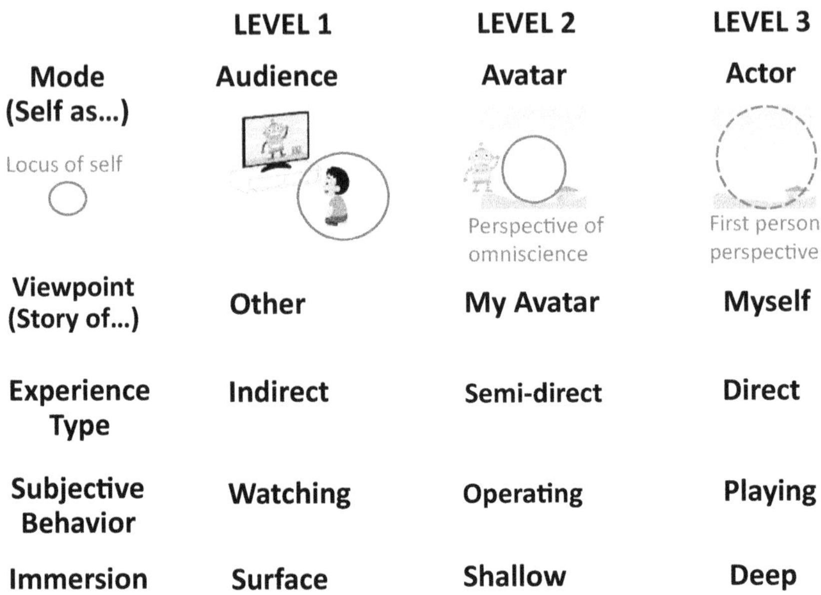

Figure 3.1 Level of Immersion in Media Experience (LIME) model.

In level 2 (Avatar mode), people experience the media through recognizing (and sometimes operating) the character as an avatar as his/her alternate identity. The level of immersion is still not deep enough; that is, it remains shallow. The type of subjective behavior is the state of watching, reading, or operating, and the type of experience is intermediate between indirect and direct. The person is experiencing a story of his/her alternation from the perspective of omniscience. For example, if an avatar was damaged in the game, the operating person may feel shocked more than just watching a TV character being damaged, as it was caused by their own maneuvering. However, that is not real damage and the operator can see the damaged avatar as the other being.

In level 3 (Actor mode), people experience the media by projecting themselves onto the character. The objective behavior is the state of watching, reading, or operating. Although it appears the same as level 2, it is not. Direct experience is a unique type of experience. As if the character was himself/herself, the person is experiencing his/her story from the first person perspective. For example, if the operator fails to manipulate the game situation, their own sight or sense of control would be lost and that should be the sense we may experience in our similar actual life, though without physical pain.

Levels 1 to 3 are a spectral range marked by rough classifications. In addition, the mode may change depending on the situational and affective condition of the person who experiences the media. However, it is considered useful as a framework for identifying discreet stages of children's media experience.

The higher the level of immersion, the more direct the experience. More immersion is likely to increase children's interest in educational content and improve the level of empathy among children. In particular, level 3 has the advantage of being self-directed because it allows the children to develop the story the way they want it to be.

In particular, when using media in bullying prevention education, it is important to understand the level of media experience of the learner; that is, children. This is because the story of the teaching material can only be considered as a thing by experiencing it as level 2 (Avatar mode) or level 3 (Actor mode) in ways that are beyond level 1 (Audience mode). The impact of bullying prevention education using the media depends on the level of children's immersion in the media. Moreover, even if the teaching material assumes level 1 so far, it is possible to raise the level of immersion in the children's media experience, depending on the ingenuity of the educator or practitioner. It may also be possible to map various practices of bullying prevention education with this LIME model. For example, practices such as watching a video or reading text may be located in level 1, and other practices may encourage children to control their own avatar, like KiVa games in the KiVa program that are located in level 2. A number of educators and practitioners may implicitly understand and intervene with this LIME model. In the future, educators will want to seek improvement of these practices based on this model and its further refinement.

Related models that elicit the LIME model

The LIME model has predecessor models for reference. One of them is "Three Layers of Personality Development" proposed by Dan P. McAdams (McAdams, 2013). He describes personality development at three levels: actor, agent, and author. I was inspired by McAdams's idea for the three modes (Audience, Avatar, and Actor). Another is the User Engagement Scale (O' Brien and Toms, 2008) as a psychometric tool to measure engagement during video game-play. Although the models overlap in terms of possessing discrete stages that are differentiated by the appearance of new modes of media interaction, there are stages, and new modes appear as they develop. Level 3 leads to a deeper level of life understanding than level 1. The model allows us to identify the status quo and lead to a deeper understanding of human interaction and self-reflection by moving to a higher level. There are many studies that refer to immersion or engagement (e.g. Kato and Igarashi, 2016; Brockmyer et al., 2009; Cairns, 2016; Jennett et al., 2008; Osanai and Kusumi, 2016).

The common point between the LIME model and the "Three Layers of Personality Development" (McAdams, 2013) is that there are three modes, each of which overlaps and deepens the understanding as a student's immersion level goes up. It is similar in that it can be used for support as well as understanding and grasping the current situation or phenomenon.

The uniqueness of the LIME model is how it explains the qualitative differences in psychological effects on media experiences from the perspective of immersive levels. The McAdams model represents the addition of modes with aging, but the LIME model does not. The LIME model shows that each of the psychological influences and the mode of media experience varies by person according to various factors such as personality and situation, even if the media experiences are the same.

The LIME model may be useful in education using media. In recent years, many children have been exposed to the media from birth, and many discussions have been held on their positive/negative effects. However, there is some debate about what they are learning through media experiences. It is inadequate to connect the kind of media as a stimulus to the influence from the media as a response in a short-circuited manner, and it is important to examine the psychological state of the subject who is experiencing the media. The LIME model provides a framework for identifying the state of people's media experience.

The McAdams model focuses on personality development, but the current LIME model does not. The LIME model focuses on the intercourse between people and media. The development of media serves as a background to the LIME model.

The LIME model seems to be the first model to explicitly indicate differences of media experiences focusing on levels of immersion, though there may be other similar models or ideas that focus on immersion or engagement in media. To explain human behavior in combination with other models, for example, a model that integrates a LIME model (audience, avatar, actor) and a McAdams model (actor, agent, author) can be considered.

Implications of the LIME model

The following three points demonstrate the utility of the LIME model. First, it positions the child's media experience; second, it positions the child's app/game use; and third, it allows us to design the child's media experiences. It is important to think about what children experience depending on the type of media. While immersion will increase interest and motivation for learning, excessive immersion can be counterproductive. Therefore, it is important for educators to understand what students experience through the media, the degree and quality of their immersion. The following chapters consider this model's effective impact on apps/games. In the discussion of the chapters, better design of future media experience for children will emerge. Further related research and development will make this LIME model more useful and practical in the future.

References

Brockmyer, J. H., Fox, C. M., Curtiss, K. A., McBroom, E., Burkhart, K. M., and Pidruzny, J. N. (2009). The development of the Game Engagement Questionnaire: A measure of engagement in video game-playing. *Journal of Experimental Social Psychology*, *45*, 624–634. doi:10.1016/j.jesp.2009.02.016

Cairns, P. (2016). Engagement in digital games. In H. O'Brien and P. Cairns (eds.), *Why Engagement Matters: Cross-disciplinary Perspectives on Engagement in Digital Media* (pp. 81–104). Berlin: Springer. doi:10.1007/978-3-319-27446-1

Jennett, C., Cox, A. L., Cairns, P., Dhoparee, S., Epps, A., Tijs, T., and Walton, A. (2008). Measuring and defining the experience of immersion in games. *International Journal of Human Computer Studies*, *66*(9), 641–661. doi:10.1016/j.ijhcs.2008.04.004

Kato, J. and Igarashi, T. (2016). The effects of narcissism and self-esteem on immersion in social network games and massively multiplayer online role-playing games. *The Japanese Journal of Psychology*, *87*(1), 1–11. doi:10.4992/jjpsy.87.14033

McAdams, D. P. (2013). The psychological self as actor, agent, and author. *Perspectives on Psychological Science*, *8*, 272–295. doi:10.1177/1745691612464657

O'Brien, H. L. and Toms, E. G. (2008). What is user engagement? A conceptual framework for defining user engagement with technology. *Journal of the American Society for Information Science and Technology*, *59*(6), 938–955. doi:10.1002/asi.20801

Osanai, H. and Kusumi, T. (2016). Reliability and validity of the narrative transportation scale in Japanese. *The Japanese Journal of Personality*, *25*(1), 50–61. doi:10.2132/personality.25.50

4 Positive use of visual media to understand and prevent bullying

The popularity and possibility of manga

Akihiko Ieshima, Yi-Shan Tsai, Brent Allison, and Tomoya Yamamoto

This chapter focuses on the impact of manga on children. Visual media such as manga, anime, and games are very popular among children not only in Japan, but also in other countries. Although such pop cultures have achieved widespread popularity worldwide, little is known about their impact on children. In particular, positive aspects are not well discussed. Therefore, it is necessary to investigate the significance of their popularity and possible impact on children. This chapter discusses the following three points: 1) the reason children are devoted to manga, 2) impact of manga on children, and 3) positive use of manga to prevent traditional/cyber bullying and other Internet-related problems. Although the most popular view of manga tends to be negative regarding the impact on child readers, we challenge this view by investigating the potential of using manga to positively influence children's well-being. This chapter discusses the recent history of manga, its current situation, and the possibility of introducing a new usage of manga to positively impact children.

Why are children devoted to visual media?

Impact of visual media on child development

Scholars' perceptions of the impact of comics on child development have changed considerably since the 1950s, when psychiatrist Frederic Wertham decried their influence in his seminal but now discredited study *Seduction of the Innocent*. In this work, Wertham (1954) argues that violence and sexuality in comics lead to juvenile delinquency and mental disorders among child readers. However, Wertham's study conflated several children's cases and exaggerated or omitted certain contextual information (Tilley, 2012). The study's impact was so great that public pressure almost forced the US Congress to regulate comics. However, the comics industry pre-empted such a move through self-censorship of sexuality and violence via its Comics Code Authority (Hajdu, 2008). Unsurprisingly, educators, scholars, and the public only entertained the idea that comics could have pedagogical or social value decades later (Berkowitz, 2011; Frey and Fisher, 2008; Gossin, 2009; Griffith, 2011; Hutchinson, 2009). Nevertheless, the idea of including comics or popular visual media in formal education is often challenged.

Note that visual media industries are not without their problems, including being sites of bullying themselves. Manga artists must often sharply curtail their artistic vision under pressure from their editors. Moreover, the Japanese animation industry is notorious for the long working hours endured by underpaid staff, a phenomenon that afflicts even those in middle management in anime studios (Morisawa, 2015). Bullying is a symptom of and contributor to embedded economic, gendered, racial, and handicapist systems of inequity. Thus, it would be a mistake to conceptualize anime and manga as an instrumental and piecemeal salve to reduce bullying while ignoring it among anime and manga creators and in deeper systems of oppression that engender the practice.

Use of comics and animation in education

In education, using comics and animation may help children realize a more robust moral vision to enact in their communities; however, this requires that educators avoid approaching it as a narrow modeling exercise that exemplifies "do and do not" behaviors. Educators often eschew didacticism (at least philosophically) for academic instruction, but are more willing to accept it as a method for teaching character education (Kohn, 1997). Fortunately, some researchers have described a range of alternative activities that incorporate animation and comics that vary widely in ways that suit most teachers' goals and pedagogical approaches.

More conservative non-didactic approaches may involve using cartoon examples of ambiguous situations of moral culpability that spur students to discuss how they (as individuals and hypothetically as peers) may respond (Leff et al., 2011). This can be especially helpful for black students in North America, who while their dissemination and receipt of overt physical bullying is acknowledged by the dominant culture, also experience less overt forms of social bullying that are not as widely recognized (Leff et al., 2011). Using more complex cartoons such as graphic novels can encourage students to more systematically conceptualize how peers from immigrant families come to know themselves as not quite fitting into the world of their families or the dominant culture (Helsel, 2018). By examining the grueling, frustrating, and conflicted process of identity consciousness and formation of immigrant-heritage protagonists (a process not unlike the adolescence of dominant culture youth), the "otherness" of their ethnic group is more likely to dissipate. Similarly, graphic novels that lack this detailed exploration of the experiences of the marginalized within systems of power (vis-à-vis gender) (Ripley, 2012; Taber and Wolshyn, 2011) may also be critically interrogated. The teacher does not need to explicitly state the implications of bullying, as this can be explored independently by the class.

Instructional methods that involve students' creation of art that mimics the conventions of visual media more readily lend themselves to the ideal of constructivist learning. They also provide instructors with a more concrete indicator of the current parameters of students' moral reasoning. Comics created by children that address interpersonal conflict are a medium through which students develop their language facilities and draw objects, sound effects, and movement to better illustrate their conceptions of justice or care (Johansson and Hannula, 2014). We recommend caution in interpretation, as physical and social bullying can be doled out in the name of justice or care (such as bullying motivated by revenge). Moreover, a student drawing of graphically violent justice meted out to evildoers or characters coming to peaceful consensus is a poor indicator of whether or not a child is likely to bully others. However, student-created comics can be an even more powerful initiator of a conversation on where morality comes from; who decides what is "moral" and why; and where the line is between justice, care, and different forms of bullying.

The popularity of manga among children

Comics in the Japanese context have been written for both entertainment and educational purposes. Japanese comics, known as *manga*, are popular among children worldwide. In Japan, manga are generally published first via comic magazines such as *Weekly Shounen Jump*, *Big Comic Original*, and *Ciao*, which publish several serial manga titles, releasing one chapter of each title in a single issue. Each manga chapter is roughly 20 to 40 pages, and the magazine comprises approximately 200 to 800 pages in total. Comic magazines are usually published every week, with exceptions such as *Big Comic Original*, which is published twice a month. The three largest publishing companies in the manga market, Kodansha, Shueisha, and Shogakukan, are almost wholly responsible for the top 50 manga magazines in circulation in Japan (Japanese Magazine Publishers Association, 2018). After being serialized through a magazine, the comics are then published in stand-alone volumes known as *tankoubon*.

Some say that the origin of manga is *Chōjū-giga*, a national treasure owned by the Kōzan-ji temple in Kyoto. *Chōjū-giga* is a Japanese illustrated narrative called *emakimono*, which is Japanese for rolling picture. *Chōjū-giga* is composed of four *emakimono*. In *Chōjū-giga*, birds and beasts are drawn like people. Yet some experts are skeptical of this discourse recently.

Manga has changed and developed over the centuries, and has a long and complicated history. Manga has various market niches because of their various categories in terms of genres, art styles, and marketable age demographics. Furthermore, some sophisticated and informative manga address topics such as politics, religion, social economics, education, and medical issues.

Manga has the following particular features: 1) manga is a visual and literary medium that significantly reduces the time it takes to read a page compared to reading a novel. However, it is not as passive as watching TV, anime, or movies. 2) the success and content of serialized manga depends on readers' response via online commenting and manga purchasing. If one manga loses popularity with readers, it is discontinued. If a sub-character becomes more popular than a main character, then they may become important characters. This differs from other media, in which viewers can evaluate the movie after they see it, but cannot affect the story. 3) manga's penchant for unrealistic, stylized, and expressive images (e.g., big eyes, long legs, physics-defying hairstyles) is known even to non-readers. However, today, some foreign comic artists also adopt the style found in manga. Because of this globalization of manga, it may be difficult to distinguish Japanese manga from foreign works in the future.

In Japan, manga is very popular and read by various people including white collar workers reading it on commuter trains, students reading during school breaks, and homebound parents reading it in the household. Manga is a big business. In 2006, the total circulation of comics and comic magazines was about 1.3 billion copies with gross sales of around USD 4.4 billion.

Because of the extensive popularity of manga, manga titles in general reflect Japanese social trends. However, little attention has been given to why people love manga so much. This phenomenon invites psychological examination based on a possible relationship between the mentality of young people and manga.

How manga became popular overseas

As a popular cultural text, manga has attracted polarized views outside Japan. In addition to the stereotype of comics as non-serious literature with a low literacy value, manga is burdened by criticisms principally directed toward its representations of violence and sex (Barker, 1989; Allen and Ingulsrud, 2005; Gibson, 2012). In 2004, the Reading Agency, a charity funded by the UK government, ran a project called Manga Mania to promote reading for leisure. They selected 150 titles to send to libraries and schools, targeting youth aged 13 to 16 years (Curzon, 2004a). The project fueled debate on the legitimacy of introducing manga to schoolchildren. For example, British News Paper, *The Mail on Sunday*, published an article titled "Child murder, incest, and rape … is this really how our schools should be encouraging boys to read?" (Curzon, 2004b). The author of this article argued that the project might lead teenagers to seek out pornographic titles once they become hooked on the text form. Although manga are created for wide demographic groups varying by gender and age, concerns about children reading the "wrong" manga and ignorance of the demographic variety in its targeted readership have resulted in calls to ban it from schools.

Regardless of the controversial nature of manga and comics in general, some scholars have tried to redirect attention from the infamous stereotypes of these texts toward a fuller awareness of their potential. For example, Meek (1988) notes that the literary competence needed to read comics is neglected. Comics demand the skill to interpret and integrate two modes of text. For example, the reader is required to comprehend the time flow of sequential panels because the linear narrative in the panels combines words and pictures to produce a type of (e)motion. Versaci (2001) highlights at least three advantages of using comic books in the classroom. First, students can explore literature in various forms. Second, students may be more forthcoming with their ideas and opinions about comic books than about traditional literary works, as the latter may be considered as occupying a space above their level of thought. Third, introducing comics in the classroom teaches students to avoid making assumptions based on the appearance or popular conceptions of certain works and genres too quickly. Gibson (2009) adds that comics can stimulate students' interest in reading and build emergent readers' confidence. Moreover, Gibson (2007) contends that a manga reader's community can enable young people to form their personal identities in relation to a subculture. Similarly, Bitz (2009) points out that achievements in the creation of comics allow fans to build up self-esteem, which while personally meaningful and rewarding to fans, is often overlooked by the dominant culture. These scholars try to point out the positive educational and social values in manga and comics that should not be overlooked.

Current situation of overseas manga

Despite dichotomous opinions in the popular discourse, manga has become a significant cultural phenomenon alongside the popularity of its side-by-side products, namely anime and games in the neighboring countries of Japan and in the Western world. In 2012, Hakuhodo (2013) conducted a global habit survey of consumers' lifestyles and media preferences in 36 major cities worldwide. The report claims that consumers in most of the cities studied prefer manga and anime to local alternatives. The phenomenon is most prominent in Hong Kong and Taipei, where 76.3% and 65.4% of comics and animations consumed were from Japan. This cultural phenomenon has also been observed in Malaysia. For example, Comic Fiesta is a convention organized by a student club, SAY Youth Society, which started with only a few hundred visitors in 2002 and expanded to nearly 40,000 visitors over a decade (Yamato, 2016). A study indicates that the market for English-translated manga grew by 350% from 2002 to 2007, peaking at an estimated USD 210 million (Brienza, 2009). Moreover, a recent publication by the Association of Japanese Animations (Masuda et al., 2018) reported that the Japanese anime market has expanded continuously since 2010 for seven consecutive years, with 110% growth on a yearly basis. In particular, the summary of the industry in 2017 shows that overseas sales continue to be the leading channel of the Japanese anime industry since the previous year, with a 131.6% increase from 2016. It concludes that overseas sales supported the overall growth of the industry (p. 3).

In Western countries, the popularity of manga and anime is particularly notable in the US and Europe. According to Goldberg (2010), manga dominated the US graphic novel market in 2007. However, the industry soon suffered a huge setback in the following years as a result of the economic recession in North America (Brienza, 2014). In Europe, the success of manga in France is particularly prominent. According to Briel (2010), manga led the sales charts for comics in France in 2007. Since the 2010s, Japanese titles have been ranked the second most translated foreign titles (following English) into French (Katelan, 2018). In 2016, 13.6 million copies of manga were sold in France, equating to one copy per five persons nationwide (Pellitteri, 2019). In 2017, 15 million volumes of manga were sold, reflecting an increase of about 9%. This was reportedly the highest sales in eight years, accounting for about 35% of the global comics sector in France (Kubo, 2018). In the UK, manga and anime have also created a transnational popular culture. They have been part of the main features in the largest comics conventions organized by MCM Comic Con held twice yearly in London and Birmingham, and annually in Manchester and Glasgow. In total, 240,000 people visited the 2018 MCM comic convention in these four cities according to the organizer's website ("Shows – MCM Central," n.d.). The popularity of manga inspired the British publisher SelfMadeHero to launch the company with a series of Shakespeare's plays in manga style under the collective title *Manga Shakespeare* (Tsai, 2016). This series endeavors to attract young readers who find it hard to read classical literature in its original form and educators who teach Shakespearian literature. The free teaching resources on the company's website clarify that these re-appropriated manga serve the purposes of entertainment and education. Underlying the decision to represent one of the greatest cultural exports of the UK in a manga style is an acknowledgment of the cultural influence that Japan has successfully wielded worldwide through this form of literature (Keener, 2015). The triumph of manga as a cultural ambassador of Japan is evident through what is claimed to be "the largest exhibition of manga ever to take place outside of Japan" (Stevens, 2018) in the British Museum at the time this chapter was written.

Reasons why manga and anime became popular in Western countries

Scholars attribute the overseas success of manga and anime to numerous factors. First, the recognition of the soft power of manga, anime, and their spinoffs has led to a series of actions by the Japanese government to legitimize the cultural status of these popular texts. A White Paper published by the Japanese government in 2000 acknowledged manga and anime as a national treasure and expressed a commitment to promote a positive image of Japan through these cultural products (Suter, 2016). This has led to the establishment of international manga awards (Schodt, 2014), the Kyoto International

Manga Museum, and implementation of the *Cool Japan* campaign (Suter, 2016). Despite criticism that manga's soft power has little impact on the ability of the Japanese government to realize policy aims (Groot, 2017), one of the unacknowledged benefits of its cultural influence is its ability to enable readers to imagine different realities and thereby inspire curiosity about Japan (Leheny, 2015).

Second, technology has greatly lifted geographic constraints. While early attempts to introduce manga to the US were set back by the opposite reading direction of the book to American readers, the success of anime through broadcasting and videotape distribution eventually eased access to it (Gravett, 2004). A similar pattern was observed in other Western countries. For example, the success of anime titles such as *Akira* and *Spirited Away* in the UK increased the success of manga, and sometimes vice versa (Hayley, 2010). As reading habits and human communications become more digitized, the Internet has become one of the main distribution channels of manga and anime. A survey revealed that sales of digital manga volumes have overtaken sales of physical copies in Japan (Pineda, 2018). However, the lagged supply of English-translated titles and immediacy of the Internet have also led to a culture of "scanlation"—a collective effort among fans to scan, translate, edit, and circulate manga or anime without a license through online channels. While this long-standing practice has positive effects on promoting manga and anime overseas through digital sharing, its damage to the overall industry is repeatedly reported (Brenner, 2007; Freedman, 2017; Kamei, 2018; Kelts, 2018).

Third, scholars have debated whether "otherness" or "Japaneseness" have drawn Western readers to manga and anime (Fennell et al., 2013; Napier, 2001). However, manga and anime are first created for the Japanese audience by Japanese artists, making Japanese cultural elements traceable from the story settings, themes, names, and characterizations (Pellitteri, 2011). This is on top of the reading direction and unique grammar of visual symbols (Brenner, 2007). In fact, foreign consumers' attraction to the unique art forms of manga and anime has led to the appearance of "how to draw manga" guides in the market and consequent growth of original English-language (OEL) manga. The appropriation and indigenization of manga-inspired art is one example of Japanese soft power and its socio-cultural impacts in Western societies. We continue discussing this popular cultural phenomenon among young readers in the UK in the next section.

What is the impact of manga on children?

Studies on manga in the UK

Based on the popularity of manga among young people in the UK, local bookstores and public libraries have set up an independent section for manga. A few schools that welcome it as an alternative reading option for children have also introduced manga to school libraries. During 2013 and 2014, one of the authors visited two schools in London where the librarians were very supportive of students' interest in non-mainstream reading including manga (Tsai, 2015). These two school libraries housed a substantial collection of manga, and clubs were held regularly for keen readers to get together and discuss or draw manga. In these libraries, excellent works from "manga drawing competitions" were hung on the walls. One of the authors spoke to 16 keen manga readers aged between 10 and 15 years about their reading experience. The participants were divided into groups by gender in each school, which resulted in a total of four groups. Each of the groups received three interviews to talk about three pre-selected manga (Naruto volume 6, Vampire Knight Volume 4, and one title of each participant's own choice). Each participant received an individual interview subsequently to talk about their overall experience as a manga fan. Some of the participants received a follow-up interview on themes that emerged during the process of data analysis. The names of the participants have been replaced by pseudonyms in this article. The results of the interviews show that these young readers engaged with manga in at least four dimensions: textual, social, emotional, and cognitive.

In the textual dimension, the interplay between words and images requires readers to actively piece together clues carefully arranged by manga artists. The fragmented nature of manga based on its sequential storytelling style and excessive use of close-up images (Tsai, 2018) further demands readers to draw "closures" (McCloud, 2001) to the undetermined meanings between panels. Moreover, the skillful interchanges between the perspectives of images figuratively stitch viewers into the narrative. In the social dimension, these readers engaged in conversations and activities such as drawing and cosplay with others sharing the same passion for manga. Furthermore, these young readers found a unique identity in the fan community, constituted by their expertise in manga, their passion for manga, and their defense of manga against external criticism (Tsai, 2016). Finally, these young readers engaged with manga characters emotionally and cognitively by immersing themselves in the fictional world, and negotiated meanings by connecting a character's experience to their own in real life. We elaborate this dimension to explain how manga could be used as a means to initiate conversations with young readers regarding their views of certain social issues.

Immersion in a book is generally described as a pleasurable experience. Csikszentmihalyi (2002) uses the analogy "flow" to describe an optimal experience of a state in which "people are so involved in an activity that nothing else seems to matter" (p. 4). The readers in this study highlighted this experience as part of the reason they enjoyed manga. In addition, to shelter themselves temporarily from worries and pressures in life and experience a sense of empowerment through a character's achievements, they gained a better understanding of the real world and insights into reality. For example, Olaf explained how he satisfied his curiosity about the world from a proximate reality in manga:

> I always want to understand how the world is, what happens in this world we live in, like how countries are, what might happen, or "Why is this happen[ing]?" "How should we react and stuff?" … The challenges they [characters] face are similar to the challenges [that] we face.

According to Olaf, the mixture of realism and fantasy in manga enabled him to enjoy the super power and learn from a character's experiences and situations that might parallel those in the real world.

Another reader, Elsa, also indicated that character development in manga taught her lessons about possible ways to react to adversities in reality:

> Say the story I read is about a girl who was raped by her friend's boyfriend … [I think about] how I can react to this, and see what they do to finish this situation.

The two examples show that young readers constantly draw on their understanding of people in reality to make sense of characters' actions. In return, the characters may bring new insights into their perception of the wider world. Cocks (2004) points out that readers weigh their prejudices, beliefs, and knowledge of what seems normal or correct in the story to decide whether the character's representation is convincing or if the development of events in the story makes sense. In this way, the proximate reality in manga provides a safe space for readers to imagine themselves in a situation that would otherwise be too difficult and harsh to deal with in reality. On the other hand, young people's engagement with manga is tied to the personal relevance they find in the story. Manga provides a set of models that allow readers to reflect on what happens in their own lives, at least to a certain extent. The elements of relevance connect the fictional to the real, enabling manga to speak to its readers in a way more entertaining than didactic.

These keen readers expressed that adults' respect for their interest in manga would help children open themselves to sharing what matters to them and how they perceive the world. When conversations about manga are scaffolded with the teacher's guidance, children can develop critical reading skills and learn about themselves. For example, Olaf reflected on his experience of participating in this manga study:

> I think the idea of talking with someone else about the way we see manga is a good idea, because normally with my friends, we talk about a certain manga or about how it is similar. We do not talk about the effect of manga and/or how it is really important, how it changes certain things about us, and how life is. I think it is really important, but I think we normally do not talk about that.

Elsa, on the other hand, was surprised by herself as a complex reader during group conversations:

> When it came out of my mouth, I was just thinking, "Really? I actually think about it like that?"

The experience of talking to children about manga raises questions about whether by barring manga from the classroom based on our concerns, we have missed a precious opportunity to let children explain to us the significance of their own reading choice. Fiona and Arthur reflected on the experience in this study:

> It is not usual that I am able to express my feelings and tell other people about [why] manga is actually important to me, and why people could relate to it.
>
> —Fiona

> It [the research project] makes me feel my hobby is not useless. Like, at least I can socialize with people about manga.
>
> —Arthur

The feedback from these young readers should prompt us to re-examine the fundamental purposes of reading. As Smith (1988) contends, "Literacy is a matter not of honing skills but of increasing confidence, familiarity, and understanding, all consequences of meaningful use" (p. 103). Despite being a non-mainstream reading material, the literary, social, and cultural value of manga, as demonstrated in this chapter, refuses the label of "inferior literature" in the populist discourse.

Studies on manga in Japan

In Japan, many studies on manga have been conducted by quasi-academics and sociologists. Some psychological studies related to manga also exist, although only in a few fields of psychology (Ieshima, 2007). In this section, we introduce some studies and provide meaningful results.

Investigating manga as a form of visual narrative, one of the authors conducted in-depth interviews, questionnaires, and used other methodologies to explore why young people like manga. The research was conducted over a period of more than 15 years. We found that the visual image unique to manga is one of the reasons young people like it. A further discovery is that young people feel that they learn more from fictitious manga characters than from their immediate environment, similar to the observation of British readers' engagement with manga mentioned in the previous section. We explain the impact of manga on young people, with reference to the survey findings.

The first survey was conducted on the web (Ieshima, 2008a). The purpose was to explore what people learn from manga in general. Research was conducted on "mixi," the biggest social network service in Japan. The name of the Internet community we focused on was: "We learned important things from manga." More than 93,000 people have participated thus far. First, we negotiated with the owner of the community and began to collect narratives. We extracted 992 narratives related to the influence of manga and analyzed them following the KJ method (Kawakita, 1967), a popular and well-known methodology used to analyze qualitative data. The main themes people learned from manga were classified into five categories: 1) what LOVE is, 2) the importance of true FRIENDSHIP, 3) EFFORT, 4) LIFE, and 5) useful/practical INFORMATION. Each has a sub-category. The psychological effects of reading manga were classified into three groups: (motivation) during the introductory phase of education, using manga will be effective in increasing students' interest and learning motivation. In addition, relaxation will help produce manga, which is fun and comfortable to read, not serious bullying. Finally, (self-reflection) if you can provide students with something to think about in relation to bullying through manga, it will help raise their awareness of bullying by increasing their self-reflection.

The second was a questionnaire survey to explore how young people read manga (Ieshima, 2008b). The participants were 300 university students in Japan (mean age = 19.3 years). Participants were required to fill out a questionnaire, which was designed to explore their personal experiences with manga. We asked them: "What is the most important thing for you when you read manga?" The responses mentioned the storyline as being most important when reading manga. Other important factors were visual image, genre, character, and general evaluation. Since more than half the participants regarded visual image as the most important factor when reading manga, it seems that both the storyline and visual image are important elements thereof.

The third was an interview study (Ieshima, 2009). The purpose was to explore what young people learn from manga. The participants were 28 university students in Japan (M = 15, F = 13, mean age = 21.4 years) and 16 university students in Chicago (M =10, F = 6, mean age = 21.5 years) who had grown up with manga. Semi-structured interviews were conducted with the participants. The interview questions were designed to explore their personal experience with manga. Examples of the questions are as follows: "Please think about your favorite manga. Which manga is the most influential for you?" "How and why do you think manga influenced you?" Each interview lasted around one hour on average. The participants compared manga with other media, and indicated that both visual appearance and characterization were key to reader identification. This was a common finding among the American and Japanese participants. However, only the former mentioned that the Japanese culture embedded in manga was attractive.

Another finding of these studies was that some Japanese readers, especially those exposed to manga since their youth, learn more about their ideal self, moral sense, knowledge, and behavior from fictitious characters (e.g., heroes and heroines) than from people in their immediate environment (e.g., parents, teachers, friends). It could be that the fictitious characters in manga become role models not only for children, but also for the youth and adults in Japan (Ieshima, 2006).

In conclusion, we emphasize the following two points. First, manga is popular in Japan and the US, and young people learn many things from them. However, we do not understand the mechanism through which this occurs. Here, the phenomenon that Japanese manga is spread beyond national borders and cultural differences needs further consideration. Their peculiar visual image may be important. Second, manga is informative and useful in the development of young people. For example, young people can narrate about themselves using manga stories and characters, which helps them better understand themselves (Ieshima, 2008c). However, the mechanism of positive influence remains a matter for further examination.

How can we use manga to support the well-being of children?

To understand and prevent bullying, *ijime* is one of the most popular themes addressed in *ijime*-manga. The purpose of *ijime*-manga is to improve understanding of bullying and prevent such behavior. The inclusion of *ijime*-manga in some Japanese textbooks shows that manga has come to be used as an educational tool in formal education.

In the 2010s, the Japanese government began emphasizing "moral education" in school, noting the need to effectively tackle bullying. Therefore, bullying prevention education is mandatory in moral education courses at every school level. Some textbooks approved by the Ministry of Education, Culture, Sports, Science and Technology (MEXT) include manga works that aim to prevent bullying.

A Japanese government-authorized textbook on moral education for junior high school students, namely *New Moral Education 1* (Watanabe et al., 2019) published by TOKYO SHOSEKI CO., LTD., uses manga as a teaching material in all grades for bullying prevention education. Each manga is approximately four to six pages long.

The manga in the TOKYO SHOSEKI textbook used as a teaching material for seventh-grade students depicts stories of perpetrating girls who ignore a certain girl in the class. The manga introduces a provocative girl who spreads social conversation. Her way of talking triggered bullying. However, in the following part of the manga, one of the perpetrators imagined how the victim was hurt, and regretted her wrongdoings. The manga describes the perpetrator's inner conflict between regret and justification.

In this manga used as teaching material, the story centers on the description of emotions and the characters are not portrayed in binary roles, in other words, as absolutely right or wrong in the moral sense. Rather than instilling objective justice, it aims to let readers empathize with various roles in an actual bullying situation. Learning to project the self onto the characters of the story and understand the sentiments and judgments regarding morals has long been emphasized in moral education in Japan. However, a brief description using 15 frames does not seem to fully depict complicated bullying situations and the justifying/denying logic around it, especially victims' sorrow.

Considering the story content and length of the manga in the textbook, the level of immersion is low, representing level 1 (audience mode) of the LIME model (cf. Chapter 3). Thus, manga seems appropriate as a textbook for junior high school students, because of a safer level of immersion.

Other ijime-*manga not in the textbook*

In Japan, many manga—in addition to those in textbooks—feature the theme of bullying, for example, "Life" (Suenobu, 2002–2009) (Figure 4.1). And there are many manga containing *ijime* scenes, such as "A Silent Voice" (Ooima, 2013–2014).

At the time of its publication, Yoshitoki Ooima's "A Silent Voice" was not included in manga magazines for boys because it portrayed the harsh bullying

Figure 4.1 "Life" (Suenobu, 2002–2009) Kodansha Ltd.

of deaf girls. Later, in consultation with the Japanese Federation of the Deaf, when it was published, it was read by various generations and became a huge hit (with great commercial success). The work begins when a deaf girl transfers to a sixth-grade elementary school class. She became a target of bullying after her class failed to win the chorus competition. In particular, male students, who are at the center of the offense, make malicious insults such as making fun of her reading a textbook aloud or breaking her hearing aids. In this work, the character and psychology of the assailants are detailed over 40 pages before the scene with the victim's encounter, and non-linguistic expressions such as other people's facial expressions and gestures are richly detailed. Many readers immerse themselves in the inner world of children involved in bullying, in the world in which they live, and where the bullying takes place.

Recently, SEEK-HELP Project which is led by Prof. Mizuno at Osaka Kyoiku University launched a website (https://seek-help.net/) to introduce helpful manga for children suffering from *ijime* or for children who want to help their friends but don't know how to do (Figure 4.2). As such, manga is considered to be useful as a media which is reachable and useful for children.

As a textbook of moral education, manga are likely to be selected based on risk avoidance in stories and illustrations. On the other hand, commercial manga is more sensational in terms of content and illustration, and usually preferred by children. Since most publishers create manga for commercial rather than educational purposes, the stories and illustrations in the publications are likely to be more sensational.

Using commercial *ijime*-manga could lead children to deeper immersion, even at level 1 in the LIME model. However, there is also the risk that students who have been bullied in the past may feel distressed when recalling their past experiences, and some children will be more susceptible to violent material. These risks may be reduced if teachers have a deeper understanding and the skills needed to manage classes when using such material.

Moreover, as certain types of manga such as "A Silent Voice" attract both child and adult readers, the contents focus more on human emotions and relationships than moral doctrines. Therefore, learning design is crucial when using such materials in bullying prevention education. For example, teachers should be prepared for diverse responses from students when prompted to reflect on a character's situation, as every student has different personal experiences. These differences could be turned into teaching opportunities if carefully planned.

Final remarks

Manga in textbooks is likely at level 1 of the LIME model in terms of immersion in reading. While using commercial manga will increase the level of immersion, this is alongside non-negligible risks. We need *ijime*-manga with high effects and low risk. How can we maximize the effects and minimize the risks in delivering manga with bullying scenes for children? This

Figure 4.2 One of the manga on “seek-help.net”.

may be possible if we avoid drawing violent scenes in the manga, for example. By changing the setting, for example, replacing characters with non-human animals—that is, setting the story in a fantasy world—we may be able to make it safer. However, research on and practice for achieving such goals is scarce, and efforts are needed to improve knowledge in this regard.

References

Allen, K. and Ingulsrud, J. E. (2005). Reading manga: Patterns of personal literacies among adolescents. *Language and Education, 19*(4), 265–280. doi:10.1080/09500780508668681

Barker, M. (1989). *Comics: Ideology, Power and the Critics*. Manchester: Manchester University Press.

Berkowitz, D. (2011). What the public really thinks about using fan fiction in the K-12 classroom: An approach using critical discourse analysis. *Paper presented to the Comics and Popular Arts Conference*, September 2, 2011.

Bitz, M. (2009). *Manga High: Literacy, Identity, and Coming of Age in an Urban High School*. Cambridge, MA: Harvard Education Press.

Brenner, R. E. (2007). *Understanding Manga and Anime*. London: Libraries Unlimited.

Briel, H. (2010). The roving eye meets traveling pictures: The field of vision and the global rise of adult manga. In M. Berninger, J. Ecke, and G. Haberkorn (eds.), *Comics as a Nexus of Cultures: Essays on the Interplay of Media, Disciplines and International Perspectives* (pp. 187–210). London: McFarland & Co.

Brienza, C. (2009). Paratexts in translation: Reinterpreting "Manga" for the United States. *International Journal of the Book*, *6*(2). Retrieved from www.academia.edu/215902/Paratexts_in_Translation_Reinterpreting_Manga_for_the_United_States

Brienza, C. (2014). Did manga conquer America? Implications for the cultural policy of "Cool Japan." *International Journal of Cultural Policy*, *20*(4), 383–398. doi:10.1080/10286632.2013.856893

Cocks, N. (2004). The implied reader. Response and responsibility: Theories of the implied reader in children's literature criticism. In K. Lesnik-Oberstein (ed.), *Children's Literature New Approaches* (pp. 93–117). London: Palgrave Macmillan. doi:10.1057/9780230523777_5

Csikszentmihalyi, M. (2002). *Flow: The Classic Work on How to Achieve Happiness*. London: RHUK.

Curzon, J. (2004a, December 07). An interview with the reading agency. *Otaku News*. Retrieved from www.otakunews.com/article.php?story=214

Curzon, J. (2004b, November 21). Mail on Sunday portray manga in a bad light. *Otaku News.* Retrieved from www.otakunews.com/Article/186/mail-on-sunday-portray-manga-in-a-bad-light

Fennell, D., Liberato, A. S. Q., Hayden, B., and Fujino, Y. (2013). Consuming anime. *Television & New Media, 14*(5), 440–456. doi:10.1177/1527476412436986

Freedman, A. (2017). Death Note, student crimes, and the power of universities in the global spread of manga. In M. McLelland (ed.), *The End of Cool Japan: Ethical, Legal, and Cultural Challenges to Japanese Popular Culture* (pp. 31–50). Retrieved from www.taylorfrancis.com/books/e/9781317269373/chapters/10.4324/9781315637884-10

Frey, N. and Fisher, D. (eds.). (2008). *Teaching Visual Literacy: Using Comic Books, Graphic Novels, Anime, Cartoons, and More to Develop Comprehension and Thinking Skills*. Thousand Oaks, CA: California Corwin Press.

Gibson, M. (2007). Manga and younger readers in Britain. Some initial observations. *IBBYLink: British Section Newsletter*. London: IBBY.

Gibson, M. (2009). The war of the worlds? Classics, comics and ways of thinking about adaptations. *NATE Classroom*, *9*, 11–13. Retrieved from www.questia.com/magazine/1G1-212851351/the-war-of-the-worlds-classics-comics-and-ways-of

Gibson, M. (2012). Picturebooks, comics and graphic novels. In D. Rudd (ed.), *The Routledge Companion to Children's Literature*. Oxford: Routledge.

Goldberg, W. (2010). The manga phenomenon in America. In T. Johnson-Woods (ed.), *Manga: An Anthology of Global and Cultural Perspectives* (pp. 281–296). London: Continuum.

Gossin, P. (2009). Interdisciplinary meets cross-cultural: Teaching anime and manga on a science and technology campus. In S. Tabachnick (ed.), *Teaching the Graphic Novel* (pp. 288–298). New York: The Modern Language Association of America.

Gravett, P. (2004). *Manga: Sixty Years of Japanese Comics*. New York: HarperCollins.

Griffith, P. E. (2011). Graphic novels in the secondary classroom and school libraries. *Journal of Adolescent & Adult Literacy*, *54*(3), 181–189. doi:10.1598/JAAL.54.3.3

Groot, G. (2017). Cool Japan versus the China threat: Does Japan's popular culture success mean more soft power? In K. Hashimoto (ed.), *Japanese Language and Soft Power in Asia* (pp. 15–41). Basingstoke: Palgrave Macmillan.

Hajdu, D. (2008). *The Ten-Cent Plague: The Great Comic-book Scare and How it Changed America*. New York: Farrar, Straus and Giroux.

Hakuhodo. (2013). Content acceptance in Asian markets driving economic growth [PDF file]. Retrieved from www.hakuhodo.jp/pdf/2013/20131213.pdf

Hayley, E. (2010). Manga Shakespeare. In T. Johnson-Woods (ed.), *Manga: An Anthology of Global and Cultural Perspectives* (pp. 267–280). London: Continuum.

Helsel, P. B. (2018). Comics and in-between kids: Immigration-themed graphic novels as a resource for second-generation adolescents. *Pastoral Psychology*, *67*, 125–139. doi:10.1007/s11089-017-0769-x

Hutchinson, R. (2009). Teaching manga: Considerations and class exercises. In S. Tabachnick (ed.), *Teaching the Graphic Novel* (pp. 262–270). New York: The Modern Language Association of America.

Ieshima, A. (2006). Influential persons in personality development. *Kyoto University Research Studies in Education*, *52*, 280–293. Retrieved from http://hdl.handle.net/2433/43761

Ieshima, A. (2007). The review and perspective of the study on manga in psychology. *Kyoto University Research Studies in Education*, *53*, 166–180. Retrieved from http://hdl.handle.net/2433/43999

Ieshima, A. (2008a). Psychological study on Japanese comics: How can we approach to manga? *The 2nd International Workshop of Multi Cultural Studies: Research Collaboration between the University of Vienna and Kyoto University.*

Ieshima, A. (2008b). Developmental change as manga reader. *19th Annual meeting of Japan Society of Developmental Psychology*, p. 364.

Ieshima, A. (2008c). Using manga in self-development support for youth. *Kyoto University Research Studies in Education*, *54*, 98–111. Retrieved from http://hdl.handle.net/2433/57036

Ieshima, A. (2009). The impact of anime/manga on personality development of youth. *Association for Research in Personality (ARP) First Stand-Alone Conference*, p. 23.
Japanese Magazine Publishers Association. (2018). Insatsu busuu kouhyou [Official announcement of the number of copies printed]. Retrieved from www.j-magazine.or.jp/user/printed/index/42/14
Johansson, J. and Hannula, M. S. (2014). How do Finnish children express care and justice in comic strips and written narratives? *Journal of Moral Education*, *43*(4), 516–531. doi:10.1080/03057240.2014.900481
Kamei, K. (2018, January 29). Pirate sites loot Japanese publishers' manga sales. *Nikkei Asian Review*. Retrieved from https://asia.nikkei.com/Business/Business-trends/Pirate-sites-loot-Japanese-publishers-manga-sales
Katelan, J.-Y. (2018, January 24). How manga conquered the world. *CNRS News*. Retrieved from https://news.cnrs.fr/articles/how-manga-conquered-the-world
Kawakita, J. (1967). *Hassoho (Abduction)*. Tokyo: Chuokoronsha.
Keener, J. (2015). Shakespeare, Manga and the pilfering of Japan's soft power. *Studies in Comics*, *6*(1), 43–59. doi:10.1386/stic.6.1.43_1
Kelts, R. (2018, May 27). Will digital piracy ruin the future of manga? *The Japan Times*. Retrieved from www.japantimes.co.jp/culture/2018/05/27/general/will-digital-piracy-ruin-future-manga/
Kohn, A. (1997). How not to teach values. *Phi Delta Kappan*, *78*, 428–439.
Kubo. (2018, February 20). Bilan de l'année manga 2017 en France: Les tops, les flops, l'état du marché ... *Manga Mag*. Retrieved from www.mangamag.fr/dossiers/bilan-annee-manga-2017/
Leff, S. S., Lefler, E. K., Khera, G. S., Paskewich, B., and Jawad, A. F. (2011). Preliminary examination of a cartoon-based hostile attributional bias measure for urban African American boys. *American Journal of Community Psychology*, *49*(3–4), 332–346. doi:10.1007/s10464-011-9461-y
Leheny, D. (2015). Naruto's limits: What soft power can actually achieve. *Nippon.com*. Retrieved from www.nippon.com/en/in-depth/a03902/naruto%E2%80%99s-limits-what-soft-power-can-actually-achieve.html
Masuda, H., Sudo, T., Rikukawa, K., Mori, Y., Ito N., and Kameyama, Y. (2018). Anime industry report 2017 summary. *The Association of Japanese Animations*. Retrieved from http://aja.gr.jp/english/japan-anime-data
McCloud, S. (2001). *Understanding Comics: The Invisible Art (1st Harper Perennial Ed edition)*. New York: William Morrow Paperbacks.
Meek, M. (1988). *How Texts Teach What Readers Learn*. Stroud: The Thimble Press.
Morisawa, T. (2015). Managing the unmanageable: Emotional labour and creative hierarchy in the Japanese animation industry. *Ethnography*, *16*(2), 262–284. doi:10.1177/1466138114547624
Napier, S. (2001). *Anime from Akira to Princess Mononoke: Experiencing Contemporary Japanese Animation*. New York: Palgrave Macmillan. Retrieved from www.palgrave.com/br/book/9780312238629
Ooima, Y. (2013–2014). *A Silent Voice*. Tokyo: Kodansha.
Pellitteri, M. (2011). Cultural politics of J-culture and "soft power": Tentative remarks from a European perspective. In M. Cornog and T. Perper (eds.), *Mangatopia: Essays on Manga and Anime in the Modern World* (pp. 209–236). Oxford: Libraries Unlimited.

Pellitteri, M. (2019). Reframing Japanese animation's success in the late 1970s: UFO Robo Grendizer at the origin of the first anime boom in Italy and France. *Journal of Italian Cinema & Media Studies*, *7*(1), 3–33. doi:10.1386/jicms.7.1.3_1

Pineda, R. A. (2018, February 28). Digital manga volume sales overtake print manga volume sales in Japan for 1st time. *Anime News Network*. Retrieved from www.animenewsnetwork.com/news/2018-02-28/digital-manga-volume-sales-overtake-print-manga-volume-sales-in-japan-for-1st-time/.128360

Ripley, D. (2012). Classroom comics: Children's medium and the new literacy. *Interdisciplinary Humanities*, *29*(1), 99–113.

Schodt, F. L. (2014). The view from North America: Manga as Late twentieth-century Japonisme? In J. Berndt and B. Kümmerling-Meibauer (eds.), *Manga's Cultural Crossroads* (pp. 31–38). New York: Routledge.

Shows – MCM Central. (n.d.). Retrieved from www.mcmcentral.net/shows/

Smith, F. (1988). *Joining the Literacy Club: Further Essays into Education*. Retrieved from www.abebooks.com/9780435100711/Joining-Literacy-Club-Essays-Education-0435100718/plp

Stevens, J. (2018, December 6). Manga exhibition to open at the British Museum in 2019. *Anime UK News*. Retrieved from https://animeuknews.net/2018/12/manga-exhibition-to-open-at-the-british-museum-in-2019/

Suenobu, K. (2002–2009). *Life*. Tokyo: Kodansha.

Suter, R. (2016). Reassessing manga history, resituating manga in history. In N. Otmazgin and R. Suter (eds.), *Rewriting History in Manga: Stories for the Nation* (pp. 175–183). New York: Palgrave Macmillan.

Taber, N. and Wolshyn, V. (2011). Dumb dorky girls and wimpy boys: Gendered themes in diary cartoon novels. *Children's Literature in Education*, *42*, 226–242. doi:10.1007/s10583-011-9131-6

Tilley, C. L. (2012). Seducing the innocent: Fredric Wertham and the falsifications that helped condemn comics. *Information and Culture*, *47*(4), 383–413. doi:10.1353/lac.2012.0024

Tsai, Y. S. (2015). *Young British Readers' Engagement with Manga* (Doctoral dissertation). University of Cambridge, UK.

Tsai, Y. S. (2016). The characteristics of manga fan communities: Preliminary observations of 16 teenage manga readers in the UK. *Journal of Graphic Novels and Comics*, *7*(4), 417–430. doi:10.1080/21504857.2016.1195759

Tsai, Y. S. (2018). Close-ups: An emotive language in manga. *Journal of Graphic Novels and Comics*, *9*(5), 473–489. doi:10.1080/21504857.2018.1480502

Versaci, R. (2001). How comic books can change the way our students see literature: One teacher's perspective. *The English Journal*, *91*(2), 61–67.

Watanabe, M., Oshitani, Y., Sasaki, T., Muto, T., Iijima, N., Isobe, T., ...Wakita, T. (2019). *New Moral Education 1*. Tokyo: Tokyo Shoseki.

Wertham, F. (1954). *Seduction of the Innocent*. New York: Rinehart & Company.

Yamato, E. (2016). "Growing as a person": Experiences at anime, comics, and games fan events in Malaysia. *Journal of Youth Studies*, *19*(6), 743–759. doi:10.1080/13676261.2015.1098769

5 Effective approaches utilizing games and apps to prevent traditional and cyberbullying

Theoretical foundation and literature review

Insoo Oh

Though many different methods have been used to reduce bullying, each method has limitations. The most representative method is to reduce violence through traditional lessons (i.e., verbal explanations). However, it is not easy to enhance students' interest and maintain their participation (Park, Jeong, and Kim, 2015). Teaching students with text-based manuals tend to make them bored. Although online education is a popular way to heighten students' interest, one-sided online lectures are less effective because they are difficult to induce interactions between teachers and students (Lee and Kim, 2016). In this chapter, we will look at the theoretical basis of the games and apps that can be used as an effective way to reduce bullying. In addition, I would like to introduce a variety of games and apps that are currently being utilized in order to explain the ways in which such games and apps work effectively.

Utilization of games: gamification and serious games

Games are being used in education in various forms. It is not just a game for fun, but it is strategically used as a way to achieve certain goals in the field of education (Kim, 2017). A technique that enhances motivation and immersion is being used by applying the principle of games to other areas such as education and rehabilitation (Lee et al., 2017; Song and Lee, 2014). This approach is called "gamification," a word which was first coined at the 2011 Gaming Summit in San Francisco. A common goal of gamification is to motivate users to have fun and act in a way that is appropriate for learning (Deterding et al., 2011). Gamification is a paradigm for solving difficult problems in non-gaming areas by utilizing a gaming mechanism. In essence, it uses a way of setting goals for the game, and then players are voluntarily complying with the rules and gaining insight through feedback. Thereby players enhance their competence in awareness, knowledge, and skills (McGonigal, 2011). There is a similar term called "serious game," which means a game designed for a primary purpose other than pure entertainment. The "serious" adjective generally refers to video games for education, scientific exploration, health care, emergency management, and city planning. The serious game shares some similarities with simulation generally, including flight simulation and medical simulation, but explicitly emphasizes the added educational value with fun and competition.

Games have been used in a wide variety of fields and have proved their effectiveness. For example, when games were applied in the area of communication, participants' communication skills were effectively enhanced (Reitz, Sohny, and Lochmann, 2019). In the case of creating virtual reality (VR) that allows players to learn a certain language in a particular situation, a game is applied to allow players to practice it. By utilizing games using VR, the participants' proficiency in using the new language was enhanced significantly and their confidence was improved through practice as well (Lin, Lan, and Kan, 2015).

Games are also known to improve relationships by building reliable rapport beyond simply improving communication skills (Kang et al., 2018). In order to improve communication between neighbors, Kang and colleagues (2018) created an app called "Everyone's Neighbour." They were able to verify its effectiveness when they found that the users of the app became much friendly and talked to each other more frequently. Jeong and colleagues (2018) also developed a "Forum VR" which was designed to enhance the cooperation of the participants since a lot of the participants were more interested in playing games than just explaining it. Furthermore, the positive effects of improving the cooperative relationships and communication skills of participants have been identified. Validation of effectiveness also confirmed improvements in intrinsic motivation and self-efficacy.

The effectiveness of games have also been proven in the field of tackling school bullying. "Stop Bullying" is a two-person scratch game developed for elementary school students. A scratch game is a game played on an equal status with the opponent. A game played without handicaps is usually applied to a typical professional golf tournament. The plot of the game revolves around overcoming school bullying from the perspective of victims and bystanders in school bullying situations. In each step, the players solve school bullying and related problems and learn proper language usage in a game format. If the players do not answer the questions properly, or if the players' score do not reach a certain level, the game ends with Friend Chip Level going down. In the final stage, if Friend Chip Level is high, the two gamer friends will get a "friendship" and be able to rescue the friend in the game. The study investigated by Lee and Hwang (2014) showed that "Stop Bullying" was effective in terms of increasing player's awareness, building friendship, and raising awareness to verbal bullying. These games allowed students to learn more about the types of school bullying and how to respond to victims and bullies appropriately. The game is highly accessible as students can enjoy it on tablets, computers and smartphones.

Limitations of using games for education

As shown above, using games has many advantages, but there are potential problems and limitations as well. The negative aspects including legal, ethical, and side effects will be discussed in the following.

Legal issues

First, legal problems can arise if a student's personal information is not protected in the use of the game as some games may collect personal information. In such cases, under the Privacy Act, the consent process for the collection and utilization of personal information should be carried out by the students themselves and their guardian (adult parents) who are their legal representatives. Due to the distinct educational purpose of the serious game, the player's personal identification data will be kept in the database. In particular, to verify the effectiveness of the serious game, information regarding the degree of achievement of the goal, learning history, access time, retention point, frequency of access, duration of the visit, number of visits, contents read, left-over (such as letters, conversations, memos, etc.), and photos/video are collected. With the use of personal identification information for individuals participating in the game, the required privacy procedures must be noted.

Second, legal problems can arise if elements of gambling are applied to serious games. In some cases, points or virtual currencies are used to heighten interest in games, and games that result in property gains or losses are strictly regulated according to law. Yi (2009) demands that it is necessary to prevent legal problems by applying preventive measures when problematic elements are present in the serious game. For example, it is recommended that the games should limit the availability of some of the acquired points in a mini-game to a limited amount of time, or limiting the size of the rewards.

Ethical problems

Ethical problems are mainly related to the methods and procedures of the game. First, the content and methods of the game should be ethical, even if the purpose of the serious game is educational. Therefore, content and methods should be justified by education experts. For example, it may not be considered favorably if a student experiences harsh bullying in the game even if it is to raise awareness of the seriousness of school bullying. There is a possibility of experiencing too much stress or trauma due to the experience of bullying in the course of playing the game. The player can also learn violent behaviors by vicariously experiencing various forms of violence which, otherwise, the players have never known.

Second, the biggest advantage of the game is the fun element, which can cause ethical problems if the fun of the game goes beyond its limits. Korhonen and colleagues (2009) said, "The fun of the game consists of challenges, competition, completion, control, discovery, exploration, self-expression, fantasy, co-consciousness, relaxation, simulation, hardship, empathy and thrill." Though it is suggested to include the above-mentioned fun factors to raise students' motivation and involvement in the game, it is necessary to discuss what kind of fun is to be allowed for educational purposes. Although the positive effects of fun are acknowledged, there are certainly hard-to-accept experiences in the application of the game. It is important to bear in mind the problem of over-indulged students seeking only fun rather than educational content.

Third, ethical problems arise when a teacher let students play the games without any educational guidance. Games cannot change the intrinsic value of learning by themselves. In other words, the fun element of the game is only to help teachers get the educational content across to the students, so the game itself cannot replace education itself. It is wrong to think that teachers do not have to intervene in the process, because the purpose of education cannot be achieved simply by playing games. Therefore, the role of teachers who want to apply the game should be specified in terms of learning goals. In addition, structural relationship between the game and lessons have to be addressed alongside with understanding of the educational content.

Side effects

The feedback and rewards provided may reduce the inherent motivation of the student (Ryan and Deci, 2000). Some students tend to be more sensitive to the rewards offered in the game than to the content of the game itself. In this regard, the rewards offered in the game may reduce the effectiveness of the game. If the player is overly sensitive and obsessed with the rewards, the game's educational function will be inevitably diminished (Hiltbrand and Burke, 2011). The ultimate purpose of the game is for a student to learn effectively through the game, to be satisfied with its achievements, and to feel the value of learning. However, being overly sensitive to trivial rewards such as virtual currency and points from the game can lead to the problem.

Review of various games for reducing bullying

In this section, the major games developed to reduce school bullying will be reviewed. This section explains what the main functions of these games are and how their effectiveness was proved. Due to the nature of the game, some information on games were taken from websites that described the game rather than the academic literature.

KiVa program

KiVa is a research-based anti-bullying program (www.kivaprogram.net/wales/kiva_game) which has been developed in Finland (Salmivalli and Poskiparta,

2012). The students learn effective coping strategies to reduce bullying. The lessons cover topics related to group interaction and respectful communication. The KiVa includes computer-based lesson as well. They are targeted specifically to the children and adolescents who have been involved in bullying as bullies, victims, and as classmates who are challenged to support the victim. The purpose of this game is to put an end to bullying. The students play the game during the lessons and/or between them (also at home if Internet is available), and students get to revisit concepts learned during the lessons and practice anti-bullying actions.

According to an analysis of the effectiveness of the KiVa program with game element, it was very effective in reducing school violence and the number of victimized students. Students who participated in the program were also found to have enhanced their relational bonding within their respective schools and showed positive results in a decrease in depression and anxiety (Salmivalli and Poskiparta, 2012).

The effectiveness of KiVa has been shown in a large randomized controlled trial in many studies (Gaete et al., 2017; Nocentini and Menesini, 2016; Williford et al., 2012). In Finland, KiVa is a sought-after program: 90% of all comprehensive schools in the country are registered KiVa schools accepting this program at the beginning (Salmivalli et al., 2013). After using the KiVa game as a universal intervention to all students, it is expected that bystanders will be able to learn how to become defenders, thereby reducing school bullying. The program helps bystanders who witness bullying play a more active role in protecting victims, not outsiders who do nothing after witnessing the bullying. Therefore, it is effective for bystanders to vicariously experience bullying situations through games and learn what reactions are more effective in those situations.

Awesome Upstander

This game is based on interactive gaming methods, which encourage students to participate. Challenges are given at various levels and attract students with interesting sound effects. As the title "Awesome Upstander" suggests, the aim is to enhance bystander's social capacity such as coping skills for responding effectively when they witness bullying. The advantage of the game is that if teachers use the game as a lesson material, they can download additional materials for their future class lessons. Parents can also download related materials for household situations. Learning how to deal with bullying effectively is the main objective. Players experience an adventure game where they have to compete in school cafeterias and restrooms to save victims from bullies. In order to successfully rescue the victim, the players must gather enough friends and confront the bully together. School bullying is caused and maintained by a power imbalance between the bullies and the victims. To eradicate bullying, the power imbalance must be reversed by collecting the power of outsiders. This game can be played free of charge on the website (www.awesomeupstander.com) and it can also be downloaded for a certain fee from the Apple App Store or Google Play.

Through the game, players understand what causes bullying and learn how to confront it when they witness bullying. It can be played in a group format such as a classroom guidance unit, so that students can acquire a variety of ideas and effectively respond to witnessed bullying based on the content of the game. Students tend to be more interested in the subject of school bullying when taught in the form of a game. By playing this game, students can find the list of "Dos and Don'ts," thereby learning how to be better upstanders, and learning about the importance of defending victims.

This game also facilitates the players' social and emotional development, because students learn how to make a difference when confronting a bully. The website introduces that this is the first game that reinforces pro-social behavior in an age-appropriate way. According to Dr. Susan Lipkins, child psychologist and leading expert in the development of "Awesome Upstander," the game was designed to set the standards for teaching elementary-aged kids how to be an upstander, a person who knows how to intervene in a bullying situation in a safe and positive manner. The game reinforces the concept of respecting and protecting others. Learning these skills during the elementary period will diminish the severity and frequency of bullying during the middle school years. Compared to other traditional approaches, a game offers a highly entertaining play style and it will be more effective when teaching them that they have the power to diminish bullying by opposing bullies together as upstanders.

Decisions That Matter

"Decisions That Matter" (https://www.andrew.cmu.edu/course/53–610/) is an interactive simulation game about bystander intervention in the situation of sexual harassment. This game was designed to allow for players to vicariously experience witnessing sexual harassment and to educate and inspire them towards primary intervention against sexual assault on college campuses. The game takes the form of an interactive graphic novel, guiding the player as a bystander through varying instances of harassment that can lead to an incident of sexual assault. The game includes five characters plus the player. For about 10 minutes, the player makes a series of decisions throughout a typical college day with friends. The player's decisions ultimately lead to a character being assaulted or not. At the end, "College of Fine Arts" actors bring the characters to life and explain their honest emotional responses to the outcome.

"Decisions That Matter" have the players educated on the situations in which sexual assault can occur. It also empowers individuals to act in different situations and make a difference with their actions. As for sexual bullying, one important component of primary prevention is effective bystander intervention (Banyard, 2013; Edwards, Rodenhizer-Stämpfli, and Eckstein, 2015).

"Decisions That Matter" addresses this head-on and allows users to really think about what they would do if they were in a situation where they had to intervene. A unique feature of the game is that the player has to make a choice out of three intermediate decisions in the game and the story develops differently depending on the decision. For example, the player has to choose one of three responses: "Say something to the stranger," "Passively dismiss the stranger," or "Ignore the stranger." In this way, the players are dynamically aware that things can unfold differently because the story's development depends on the player's decision.

"Decisions That Matter" is both a computer game and a powerful lesson in how you can protect yourself and your friends from sexual harassment. It has the advantage of vicariously experiencing the real world of sexually violent situations and learning how to apply the right coping skills as the role of a friend who witnesses them. The part of the game that resonates with the players the most is the honest expression of the characters' feelings about the situation as the cartoon-style characters turn into real people at the end of the game. This allows players to realize the impact of their decision on the other party depending on how they behave in the situation of violence. Also, if the players enter their names at the beginning of the game, the player can immerse themselves in the story because the characters call the player by his or her real name on the screen.

Review of various apps for reducing bullying

Recently, more and more attempts are being made to reduce school violence through various types of smartphone apps other than games (Cho and Kim, 2015). The purpose of the app also varies to include reporting violence, educating parents about the seriousness of bullying, monitoring their children's use of smartphones, and using them for classroom lessons. This section explains the main functions of these apps and how their effectiveness was proved. Due to the nature of the apps, some information on the apps were taken from websites that described the apps rather than the academic literature.

STOPit

A student with this app can send information on bullying anonymously to people who can provide help for victims. When this app is installed in a smartphone, it has the advantage of using the "built-in STOPit" messenger to establish a communication system that allows for two-way interaction between the parties (e.g., teachers, parents, or police-officers) in real time. Students who witness bullying need courage to report it to adults, because of the fear of becoming the next target if their identity is exposed (Lee and Kim 2018). However, such an anonymous reporting app has the advantage of reducing such fear and making it easier to report the bullying. If the bullying incident is reported to the administrator, the administrator can manage bullying incidents via the app. For example, the administrator can follow up on incidents, send out broadcast notifications, as well as generate analytics and trend report.

The reason why this app is effective is that not only the victims of bullying but also the bystanders who witnessed it can safely report the bullying to school officials to prevent the spread of the bullying. In addition to being able to send messages, they can also send photos and videos, which can be used as evidence needed to resolve disputes over future bullying. Using this app, students can easily identify and report hidden bullying cases that are difficult for school administrators to identify, which in turn suppresses the bullies' violent behavior. The bullies' aggressiveness is inhibited by the fact that anyone who witnesses their violent behavior can report it anonymously anytime and anywhere.

According to a report on the webpage, the app is currently used by 25 million people and 1,000 conversations per week are conducted via messenger. It has the advantage of making schools safer by reporting and intervening on various safety problems (including school violations, property damage, and hazardous situations) that can occur in schools. STOPit Messenger has the advantage of providing more detailed information and obtaining immediate answers and solutions by enabling real-time and two-way communication with school officials and the parties involved.

KnowBullying

This app helps parents and children initiate meaningful conversations regarding bullying (Figure 5.1). It allows for parents to have regular time for various conversations with their children, including bullying. It also has the function to share successful anti-bullying strategies on Facebook, Twitter, email, or text. Normally, students tend not to report bullying to adults when they are subjected to do so (Englander, 2013). They tend to regard reporting to adults as an act of tattling, and believe that reporting to adults will not improve situation (Kim and Shin, 2015). In practice, however, active intervention by adults, such as teachers and parents, is known to be very effective to improve bullying situations (Veenstra et al., 2014).

Conversation can be the first step in preventing bullying. If parents talk to their children about bullying for 15 minutes a day, they are more likely to ask their parents for help and advice. By sharing various information related to bullying through dialogue, it can help parents increase parental sensitivity to bullying as well. Not only that but both parents and teenagers can learn a variety of strategies to cope with bullying as well as enabling parents to help their children enhance awareness. Furthermore, it allows the students to avoid bullying as well as helping them recognize it when they witness it and act as a defender.

The app was developed by the Substance Abuse and Mental Health Services Administration (SAMHSA) from the U.S. and it is available free

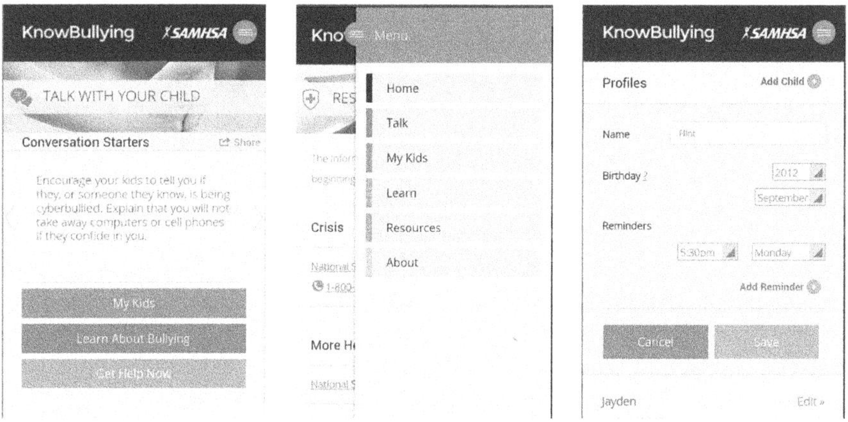

Figure 5.1 Captured smartphone screen of "KnowBullying" app.

of charge. The app provides parents and guardians with information about bullying and cyberbullying and provides a platform for them to talk about bullying with their children. It also provides information on how to prevent bullying and support victims in classrooms for teachers. This app has the advantage of nurturing a culture of schools and families to prevent bullying. More information on this app is available at the following: YouTube: https://youtu.be/x_NkNl3OfXU

My Mobile Watchdog

Originally, this app was developed to protect children from the various dangers of cyberspace. The app warns the parents the moment a stranger contacts their children or when their children receives harmful messages. In addition, parents can monitor their children's text messages, social media conversations, and phone calls, as well as track their children's locations. Due to the nature of the app, most children may show a strong reluctance to use it since it monitors their online interactions. It must be said that parents' coercive monitoring of their children can have side effects. For the app to be effective, it is necessary for children to fully understand that protecting themselves from the harmful cyber environment is the main purpose of this app. In addition, it is crucial to determine the level of use of the app through conversation so that the customization protects the privacy of the children and their rights as well as keeping their resistance to a minimum.

Since the children know that their cyber behavior is being monitored, the risk of behavior such as cyberbullying can be suppressed. In addition, due to the location tracking function, endangered children can be instantly intervened in situations where cyberbullying is suspected, thereby increasing student safety. It has the advantage of being able to collect text messages and mobile photos so they can be used as legal evidence. If the victim also warns the bullies that inappropriate message-sending behavior is being monitored, they are more likely to inhibit aggressive behaviors. By strengthening these monitoring functions, students have advantages in terms of preventing bullying in advance and controlling their behavior by utilizing self-regulation capabilities.

Improving self-regulation by using monitoring function increases positive online behavior and enhances cyber etiquette (Leonard et al., 2018; Patel et al., 2019). These apps also help create a safe cyber culture by continuously monitoring cyber-related behavior and tracking down and punishing those who repeatedly display aggressive behaviors. The app is developed by mobile security firm eAgency Mobile Security and supports Android and iOS devices, but some features do not work on iPhones. It must be noted that apps that monitor student activity by third parties usually do not work on iPhones. On the other hand, parents should keep in mind that this type of monitoring app could undermine the trust between parent and child relationships. Teenagers develop autonomy and independence during the adolescent period, so parent's forceful monitoring could threaten the relationship between parents and their children. Therefore, it is desirable to have sufficient conversation with the child and customize the level of monitoring according to the child's needs.

References

Banyard, V. L. (2013). Go big or go home: Reaching for a more integrated view of violence prevention. *Psychology of Violence*, *3*, 115–120. doi:10.1037/a0032289

Cho, H. J. and Kim, J. M. (2015). Development of conversion smart monitoring app for elementary school student. *Journal of Digital Convergence*, *13*(4), 211–217. doi:10.14400/jdc.2015.13.4.211

Deterding, S., Dixon, D., Khaled, R., and Nacke, L. (2011, September). From game design elements to gamefulness: Defining "gamification." In *Proceedings of the 15th International Academic MindTrek Conference: Envisioning Future Media Environments* (pp. 9–15). doi:10.1145/2181037.2181040

Edwards, K. M., Rodenhizer-Stämpfli, K. A., and Eckstein, R. P. (2015). Bystander action in situations of dating and sexual aggression: A mixed methodological study of high school youth. *Journal of Youth and Adolescence*, *44*(12), 2321–2336. doi:10.1007/s10964-015-0307-z

Englander. E. K. (2013). *Bullying and Cyberbullying: What Every Educator Needs to Know*. Cambridge: Harvard Education Press. doi:10.5860/choice.51-6293

Gaete, J., Valenzuela, D., Rojas-Barahona, C., Valenzuela, E., Araya, R., and Salmivalli, C. (2017). The KiVa antibullying program in primary schools in Chile, with and without the digital game component: Study protocol for a randomized controlled trial. *Trials*, *18*(1), 75. doi:10.1186/s13063-017-1810-1

Hiltbrand, T. and Burke, M. (2011). How gamification will change business intelligence. *Business Intelligence Journal*, *16*(2), 8–16.

Jeong, J. Y., Kim, S. K., Park, S. J., Jang, J. T., and Kim, S. R. S. (2018). Design and verification of VR gamification contents for cooperative thinking. *Journal of Digital Contents Society*, *19*(5), 853–860. doi:10.9728/dcs.2018.19.5.853

Kang, S. H., Jeong, J. Y., Park, S. J., and Kim, S. K. (2018). Communication effects of gamification app: Focused on "Everybody's Neighbor." *Journal of Digital Contents Society*, *19*(7), 1245–1251. doi: 10.9728/dcs.2018.19.7.1245

Kim, H. S. and Shin, K. I. (2015). Understanding for bystanders about bullying in middle school: Q-methodological approach. *Social Science Research Review*, *31*(4), 359–377. doi:10.18859/ssrr.2015.11.31.4.359

Kim, S. K. (2017). *Gamification of Learning*, Seoul: Hongreung Publishing Company.

Korhonen, H., Montola, M., and Arrasvuori, J. (2009, October). Understanding playful user experience through digital games. *International Conference on Designing Pleasurable Products and Interfaces, 2009*.

Lee, A. R. and Kim, H. Y. (2018). A study of witnesses' experiences to prevent from school violence. *Korean Journal of Sports Science*, *27*(3), 869–882.

Lee, E. H. and Kim, K. A. (2016). A needs analysis for the development of a virtual educational program for anti-cyberbullying. *Studies on Korean Youth*, *27*(3), 67–96. doi:10.14816/sky.2016.27.3.67

Lee, S. M., Kim, Y. R., Kang, B. K., and Koo, Y. R. (2017). Using gamification to motivate online learners: A study on mobile applications for language learning. *Korean Society of Design Science*, 70–71. doi:10.14816/sky.2016.27.3.67

Lee, Y. I. and Hwang, S. J. (2014). Research for prevention of school violence: Two player scratch game 'Stop Bullying'. *The Korean Association of Computer Education, 18*(1), 195–198.

Leonard, N. R., Casarjian, B., Fletcher, R. R., Prata, C., Sherpa, D., Kelemen, A., Rajan, S., Salaam, R., Cleland, C. M., and Gwadz, M. V. (2018). Theoretically-based emotion regulation strategies using a mobile app and wearable sensor among homeless adolescent mothers: Acceptability and feasibility study. *JMIR Pediatrics and Parenting*, *1*(1), e1. doi:10.2196/pediatrics.9037

Lin, T. J., Lan, Y. J., and Kan, Y. H. (2015). Research trends of language learning in virtual reality from 2003 to 2012: A content analysis. In Dickson K. W. Chiu, Minhong Wang, Elvira Popescu, Qing Li, Rynson Lau, Timothy K. Shih, Chu-Sing Yang, and Demetrios G. Sampson (eds.), *Advances in Web-based Learning –* ICWL 2013 Workshops (73–81). ICWL 2013. *Lecture Notes in Computer Science*, vol.8390. Berlin, Heidelberg: Springer. doi:10.1007/978-3-662-46315-4_8

McGonigal, J. (2011). *Reality is Broken: Why Games Make Us Better and How They Can Change the World.* New York: Penguin. doi:10.5860/choice.49-0680

Nocentini, A. and Menesini, E. (2016). KiVa anti-bullying program in Italy: Evidence of effectiveness in a randomized control trial. *Prevention Science*, *17*(8), 1012–1023. doi:10.1007/s11121-016-0690-z

Patel, M. L., Hopkins, C. M., Brooks, T. L., and Bennett, G. G. (2019). Comparing self-monitoring strategies for weight loss in a smartphone app: Randomized controlled trial. *JMIR Mhealth and Uhealth*, *7*(2), 372–390. doi:10.2196/12209

Park, Y. M., Jeong, J. W., and Kim, E. J. (2015). A study on present situation of violence in school and improvement program. *The Korean Society of Disaster Information*, *11*(1), 9–22. doi:10.15683/kosdi.2015.11.1.9

Reitz, L., Sohny, A., and Lochmann, G. (2019). VR-based gamification of communication training and oral examination in a second language. In M. Khosrow-Pour (ed.), *Computer-Assisted Language Learning: Concepts, Methodologies, Tools, and Applications* (pp. 811–828). Hershey, PA: IGI Global. doi:10.4018/978-1-5225-7663-1.ch038

Ryan, R. M. and Deci, E. L. (2000). Self-determination theory and the facilitation of intrinsic motivation, social development, and well-being. *American Psychologist*, *55*(1), 68. doi:10.1037/0003-066x.55.1.68

Salmivalli, C. and Poskiparta, E. (2012). Making bullying prevention a priority in Finnish schools: The KiVa antibullying program. *New Directions for Youth Development*, *2012*(133), 41–53. doi:10.1002/yd.20006

Salmivalli, C., Poskiparta, E., Ahtola, A., and Haataja, A. (2013). The implementation and effectiveness of the KiVa anti-bullying program in Finland. *European Psychologist*, *40*(4), 347–365. doi:10.1027/1016-9040/a000140

Song, S. I. and Lee, J. M. (2014). The effects of game program on depression and self-efficacy, rehabilitation motivation for stroke patients. *Journal of Special Education & Rehabilitation Science*, *53*(3), 133–153. doi:10.15870/jsers.2014.09.53.3.133

Veenstra, R., Lindenberg, S., Huitsing, G., Sainio, M., and Salmivalli, C. (2014). The role of teachers in bullying: The relation between anti-bullying attitudes, efficacy, and efforts to reduce bullying. *Journal of Educational Psychology*, *106*, 1135–1143. doi:10.1037/a0036110

Williford, A., Boulton, A., Noland, B., Little, T. D., Kärnä, A., and Salmivalli, C. (2012). Effects of the KiVa anti-bullying program on adolescents' depression, anxiety, and perception of peers. *Journal of Abnormal Child Psychology*, *40*(2), 289–300. doi:10.1007/s10802-011-9551-1

Yi, C. H. (2009). Improvement to ethical social environment in online games for youth. *Journal of Korea Society of Computer Games*, *17*, 151–157.

6 Development of a cyberbullying prevention game "Angry Daddy"

Hyung Sup Yoon

Background and motive for the development of the game

Korean high-speed Internet infrastructure began to be established in 1998, and, by 2018, the Internet usage rate was the highest in the world, at 91.5% of the population (Korea Internet and Security Agency, 2019). This environment proved to be a turning point for school violence as it provided a new medium where bullying could emerge: cyberbullying. The recent rapid increase of Internet and smartphone usage by South Korean students led to serious social problems, which are sometimes regarded to be cybercrimes (although students are not usually legally punished because of being underage). While school violence has continued to decrease since 2012, cyberbullying has continued to increase (see Chapter 2 for more details). The types of bullying have also become subtle and hard to detect, making it very difficult to monitor invisible cyberbullying (Lee, Kang, and Lee, 2015).

Lessig (2006) provides a summary of legal and educational responses to cyberbullying. He stressed that a more effective way to deal with cyberbullying may be to use the new technology. Kim (2011) also suggested that the effectiveness of the educational intervention will be maximized when students are familiar with the type of intervention, for example by using games. To meet such social demands, the National Information Society Agency (NIA) of Korea decided to develop an interactive educational game to prevent cyberbullying among teenagers, an age group that looks favorably at games as a medium of learning.

The game simulates interactions between bullies and victims in the game. As such, the first step in developing the game was to collect victims' effective responses to bullies' subtle aggressive words in cyberspace. A scenario was created in order to explain cyberbullying situations to players. By being exposed to a bully's attack in a virtual situation, the game allows the players to learn effective responses to bullying. While collaborating with cyberbullying prevention experts, we studied the causes, coping strategies, domestic and international cases, and various countermeasures. It was rather difficult to integrate all the different aspects into the game as it is impossible to reflect all of these cases and countermeasures.

The development procedure can be summarized as follows:

1. Collecting evidence and cases from research papers on cyberbullying;
2. Interviewing experts in the field of cyberbullying;
3. Generating scenarios based on the various cases;
4. Selecting appropriate scenarios based on students' feedback;
5. Reviewing the appropriateness of the scenarios in a Focus Group Interview;
6. Drafting a flow chart of the game based on the scenarios;
7. Integrating graphic resources, sound data, etc. into the game;
8. Conducting a play test;
9. Correcting bugs and problems found in the play test until completion.

The goal of the game is to learn effective responses in cyberbullying situations. In a cyberbullying situation, the victim's initial response is critical. After reviewing previous studies and consulting with experts, we set up the direction of the game design. The game involves a cyberbullying situation that emerges during interactive simulation (chatting). Accordingly, questions (bullying) and appropriate answers (responses) were created for each type of bullying. Counseling and educational experts in school violence were consulted when developing scenarios for each situation. The questions were elicited from actual cases which were collected in FGI (Focus Group Interview). In addition, to verify the appropriateness of the questions, graduate students conducted in-depth interviews with middle school students. Inappropriate situations and questions were excluded based on the results.

The process of developing the game "Angry Daddy"

Concept design

This educational game was designed to prevent extreme situations, as any initial verbal attack can lead to school violence or cybercrimes. By providing opportunities for teenage students to participate in a conversational simulation game, we aimed to teach the players to learn effective responses to verbal attacks. In the LIME model, Angry Daddy is based on level 2 (Avatar mode). Players are exposed to verbal attacks in cyberspace. However, the players are not directly attacked, as this might cause them to suffer psychological damage during the game. Rather, the players are placed in the position of the father of the victim under attack. This is reflected in the title of the game: Angry Daddy. Although it is presented as a form of protecting a child from a father's point of view, a verbal attack naturally puts the players in the victim's position. While playing games, the players learn how to respond effectively to virtual bullying. Since this game is based on level 2 of the LIME model, there are advantages that can reduce psychological pain caused by direct damage, and increase interest as they have a virtual experience from a father's point of view. This game is mainly targeted at middle school students who are more likely to face cyberbullying than elementary and high school students.

Analysis of previous research and cases

There have been attempts to develop a simple quiz-type game or a defense-type game but nothing had been developed in this role-play format. Analysis of these previous attempts showed that their educational effectiveness was insufficient. We reviewed three games: DIGIZEN, Cyberbully Zombies Attack and Star Stone. First, DIGIZEN is a kind of dialogue-based quiz game. This game follows on from the cyberbullying film "Let's Fight It Together" to personalize and reinforce learning through that film. This game allows users to create their own characters who go into the school where cyberbullying has taken place. Second, Cyberbully Zombies is a simple shooting game sponsored by the National Center for Missing & Exploited Children. Third, Star Stone was designed to prevent school violence with the support of Korea's Game Promotion Center. The players choose their characters and have adventures in a virtual reality village. Although the intention of developing such games was admirable, the games were not evaluated as effective due to the lack of fun, which is a critical element in games. All three games present simple quiz questions and the user should select one of two options, true or false. The players interact with simple animation feedback in the game, but evaluation analysis revealed that they lack gaming elements and that their educational effectiveness was also far below the expected level.

Therefore, we simulated a situation where the potential game users (middle school students) are attacked verbally by their peers in cyberspace, and made them practice selecting effective responses to the verbal attacks. We focused on providing fun with an interesting and interactive gaming method. The overview of the game planning is shown in Table 6.1.

Table 6.1 Overview of the "Angry Daddy" game

Genre	*Quiz-based educational game*
Concept	Students (players) play the game from the perspective of a father who tries to help his son or daughter (who is a victim of cyberbullying)
Goals	To prevent an extreme violence situation
Target group	• Main target group: middle school students • Sub-target group: higher graders in elementary school and lower graders in high school
Platform	Web browser game
Graphic	2D casual style
Play time	15–20 minutes
Supervisor	A professional counselor or classroom teacher

In order to develop an educational game that provides a more effective preventive education, we applied the following methods in our planning. First, we customized the Comebacks expressions (Lohmann and Taylor, 2013) developed in the U.S. in order to reflect the situation in Korea; "Comebacks" are verbal expressions that victims make quickly and tactfully in response to a bullies' verbal attack. "Comebacks" offers the only simple way to respond quickly to certain bullying situations. Second, we restructured bullying scenarios as a type of chat-like conversation by developing questions and answers; and third, we sought advice from experts in various fields (experts in criminology, education, and youth counseling) in order to ensure content validity.

The following features were included to enhance the game's educational effectiveness:

1. Conversational format: The application of "Comebacks" was based on a chat-like conversational format where the users participate by structuring an virtual cyberbullying situation. The Comebacks format is a one-to-one response format which demonstrates the effective response to a certain situation, but in reality, bullying happens in a more complicated and repetitive form. Therefore, we adopted a chatting type.
2. The second-best system: The second-best system was designed to enhance the user's ability to respond effectively to various situations and to make it possible to select the best and the second-best options depending on the context. This provides an opportunity for the players to experience, in advance, various ways in which to respond wisely when he/she actually faces such a situation.
3. The retry function for effective implementation of repetitive learning: Users can play the game repeatedly, however, educational games generally avoid repetition. Therefore, the replay function for repetitive learning was programed to be possible only when the player recorded a low score. Players who record a high score can immediately finish the game.
4. Prompt interactive feedback and evaluation system: The weakness of educational games lies in the fact that feedback is not given promptly or is ambiguous (Salen and Zimmerman, 2004). To overcome this weakness, a prompt audiovisual feedback system was adopted. Moreover, an evaluation system was added, which displays the level reached by the player.

Generating conversational quiz questions

Players need to know the context before selecting an effective response to a bullying message. As such, an explanation of the situation is presented at the beginning, so that the player can understand the context. Then, initial conversations between the perpetrator and the victim are presented so that the players can understand the context in detail. After the players respond, the perpetrator's reactions are shown so that the players easily understand the

Table 6.2 Examples of three types of response to cyberbullying

Response type	*Example*
Aggressive response	Do you want to fight with me? Do you really want to be beaten?
Passive response	If you hate me so much, I will disappear …
Assertive response	Maybe you're just kidding, but it still hurts me. Stop doing this.

effectiveness of their own responses. At the end of the game, an explanation of the result of the player's choice is presented to the players. If the player's response is effective, the score goes up, but if the response is ineffective, the score goes down.

The game provides three contexts, based on types of bullying: slandering type, extortion type, and excluding type. The slandering type depicts bullies speaking ill of the victim or spreading rumors to humiliate the victim. The extortion type depicts the violence of bullies forcibly taking what others have by using their dominance. The exclusion type depicts the bullies ostracizing the victim or rejecting the victim from their group by turning other members of the group against the victim. Responses of the victim are mainly classified as: "aggressive response," "passive response," and "assertive response." Examples of these three types of response are described in Table 6.2.

An aggressive response is retaliatory and impulsive, and it appears ineffective as it further provokes the perpetrator's anger. A passive response is also ineffective, as it retains the imbalance of power between the victim and the perpetrator. If the players choose one of the aggressive or passive responses, the players will immediately know their responses were ineffective because their scores will go down. On the other hand, an assertive response is effective, as the victim clearly expresses their own emotions and explicitly states what he/she wants while trying to avoid hurting the feeling of others.

Game play flow chart

The flow chart of Angry Daddy was structured as follows. The player can select the game play on the first page of the game that is configured as an angry father looking at his daughter's smartphone, which provides the player with an idea about the background of the game.

1. The game is designed to enable the player to select his/her age and gender so that the game result can be used for further research.
2. Web toons (web-based cartoon) are used in the introductory part of the game so that young players can easily understand the game situation.
3. The main game page is played repeatedly. Virtual cyberbullying situations are presented and the players try to cope with the verbal attack by responding effectively.

4. The responses are evaluated with three grades: A, B, and C. These grades are displayed in the result page. If the result is A or B, the player can choose to "play again," or to finish the game, but if the score is low, the player is automatically invited to play the game again. It is designed to improve the effectiveness of learning through repetition.

Figures 6.1 through to 6.4 show these processes in sample pages of the game. You can also watch a YouTube video that demonstrates the game through the following link: https://youtu.be/cPUoRH451RI

Feedback on play results

In order to enhance the educational effectiveness of the game, explanatory feedback is provided right after the game is completed. Therefore, the players can enhance their coping skills in regards to cyberbullying.

Analysis of the educational effectiveness of the game

Demonstration at an exhibition and survey results

The "Open Play Day," an "indie game event," is a show case event that displays indie games to be released in the near future, featuring the games being displayed for trial purposes. Developers who display games can learn how to improve their games through participants' feedback. The Angry Daddy game was displayed at the event in 2014, before its development was completed, and was offered to the audience for a test run. A survey was conducted at the event. The survey questions were classified into the following five areas: 1)

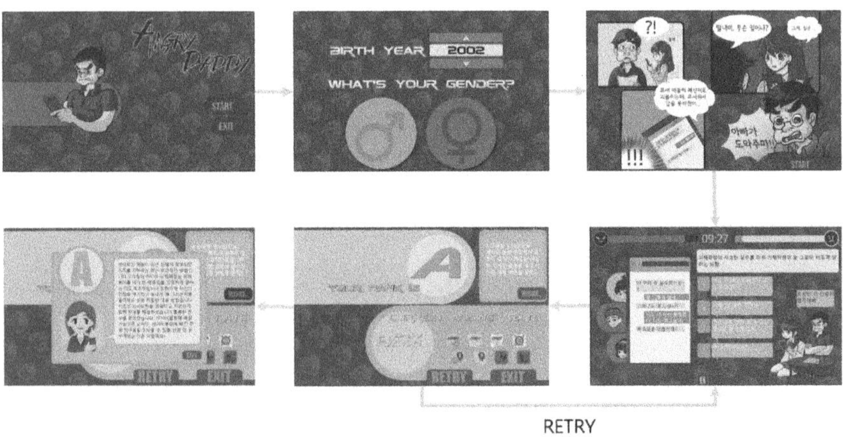

Figure 6.1 "Angry Daddy" game progress flow chart.

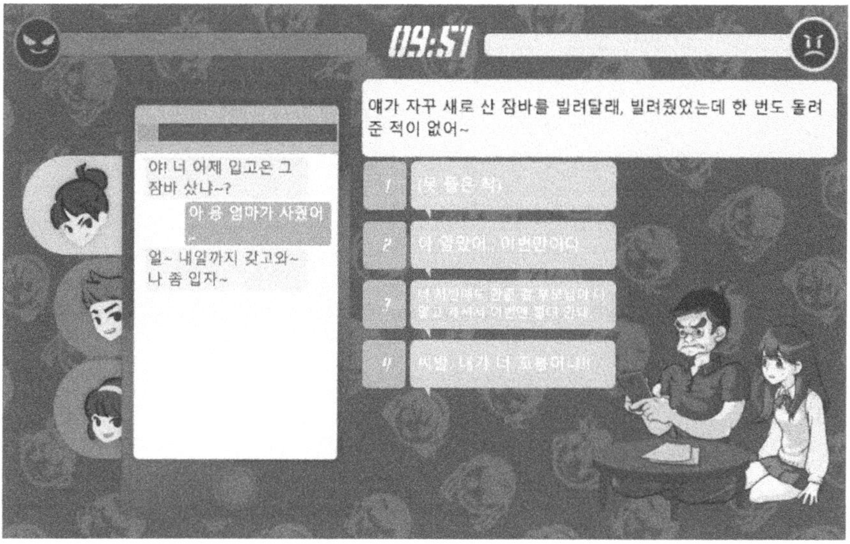

Figure 6.2 Bullying situation description and initial attack and response.

Figure 6.3 Interactive play in a virtual cyberbullying situation.

demographic information of the participant (gender, age group, experience of cyberbullying), 2) effectiveness of the game (Questions 1–4), 3) game play (Questions 5–8), 4) functions of the game (Questions 9–10), and 5) educational environment (Questions 11–14).

Figure 6.4 Personal feedback on the player's result.

According to the analysis of the responses, the game scored very highly on most of the criteria. In particular, questions regarding the "effectiveness of the game" and "game play" received very high scores. Angry Daddy was expected to have high educational effectiveness in preventing further cyberbullying by increasing players' coping skills with respect to cyberbullying. However, responses to the questions regarding "functions of the game" were somewhat unsatisfactory. In particular, scores for the function of "retry" were low, indicating that this function needs to be improved. Accordingly, the retry part was revised so that players who recorded lower scores could end the game.

The most surprising result of the analysis was about the effectiveness. In answer to what kind of educational method would be the most effective in preventing cyberbullying, 92.3% of the respondents answered that games would be the most effective. This result confirmed that the users preferred game-based learning to traditional formats such as video clips, textbooks, and special lectures. With this preliminary survey, we confirmed that using this game as a form of learning would be very effective.

Analysis of a school field test and survey results

After the first test for the general public, we conducted a second play test mainly with the target audience of the game. After conducting the play test, a survey was carried out: this play test was administered in one elementary school; 39 sixth-grade students participated; and the questionnaire was constructed in the same format as the preliminary survey.

The results of the analysis were as follows (figures refer to average scores): the item asking "how the game enhanced players' coping skills with cyberbullying" scored 4.18 points out of 5.0; the score for "increased confidence to cope effectively with similar situations in real life" was 4.20 points; the item asking if "this game was more interesting than any other educational methods" scored 3.46 points; the item asking about their "intention to recommend this game to other friends" recorded 3.97 points. The previous two items suggest that the game would be interesting and worth recommending to others. Moreover, intuitive understanding of game play recorded 4.28 points, understanding of user interface recorded 4.08 points, appropriateness of game play time recorded 3.87 points, and similarity to the actual cyberbullying situation recorded 3.92 points. Overall scores for all of the questions were high. Based on these results, it was inferred that there were no serious potential problems in using the game. As for the question asking "the retry function was effective," it was evaluated at 3.92 points.

Regarding the appropriate place for playing the game, school was selected by 46% of the respondents, followed by online (23%), home (18%), and counseling room (13%). Answers to the question regarding the most appropriate school level for this game were elementary school students (46%, 4th–6th graders), followed by middle school students (41%), elementary school students (8%, 1st–3rd graders), and high school students (5%).

Development of a manual for teachers

For educational games used in schools, a manual for teachers is essential. This is because many middle school teachers are less competent in using smart devices than their students are. Therefore, the quality of the manual for teachers is critical as it contains detailed figures and descriptions. The manual was developed as a downloadable PDF file format, so that teachers can use it during their teaching. The teacher's manual consists of 68 pages and contains various figures and explanations to help teachers understand the procedure of the game. It is structured as follows: 1) Introduction to the program, 2) How to play the game, 3) How to apply the game to classroom settings (guidance on various teaching and counseling methods for victims), 4) Detailed procedures for implementing the program, and 5) Description of the concept, questionnaire, interpretation for teachers, and effective conversational method for cyberbullying.

Comments on game development

Over the course of the development, collaboration with external experts was helpful in increasing the quality of the game. Moreover, through the play test process, feedback from teenagers was valuable in developing the procedure.

As a result of this research, the following conclusions have been drawn. First, collaboration with content experts and game development experts is essential in order to develop a good educational game. Second, the validity of the content and the format should be verified through the results of play testing by the target audience. Third, to apply the game to the appropriate field, it is essential to produce a manual for teachers. Fourth, it was confirmed that games are an effective educational tool when approaching sensitive topics such as cyberbullying as they effectively capture the attention of their audience while fostering motivation. However, this research has its limitations as well. The design of the game and its effectiveness should have been verified with more play tests in the field. Any shortcomings will be corrected by implementing more play tests and seeking more feedback.

References

Kim, B. S. (2011). Current status of cyberbullying among teenagers. In National Information Society Agency (eds.), *Violence Without Voice, Cyber Bullying Diagnosis and Solution* (pp. 13–26). Seoul: National Information Society Agency.

Korea Internet and Security Agency. (2019). *2018 Survey on the Internet Usage.* Naju: Ministry of Science and ICT.

Lee, S. H., Kang, J. H., and Lee, W. S. (2015). *A Study on the Types and Countermeasures of Youth Cyber Violence*. Seoul: Korean Institute of Criminology.

Lessig, L. (2006). *Code and Other Laws of Cyberspace*. New York: Basic Books.

Lohmann, R. C. and Taylor, J. V. (2013). *The Bullying Workbook for Teens: Activities to Help You Deal With Social Aggression and Cyberbullying.* Oakland, CA: New Harbinger Publications, Inc.

Salen, K. and Zimmerman, E. (2004). *Rules of Play: Game Design Fundamentals.* Cambridge, MA: MIT Press.

7 The application of anti-bullying smartphone apps for preventing bullying in South Korea

Insoo Oh

Smartphone apps provide new platforms for students to cope with bullying more effectively. Recently, a variety of anti-bullying smartphone apps have been developed to decrease bullying. This chapter introduces two types of anti-bullying apps which have been widely used in Korea. The first is "117 Chat" which is a secured reporting app for students to notify a bullying situation to a school police officer. "117 Chat" was developed by Metropolitan Police Agency and it has been used since 2013 in Korea. It also provides victims with 24-hour chatting services. The second is the "Cyberbullying Vaccine" in which people virtually experience cyberbullying as the victims, so that they recognize the significant impact of cyberbullying. The users are cyberbullied by three types of bullying such as Kakao Talk, Facebook, and smartphone message. These apps help people realize the significant impact of cyberbullying, so that they become active agents to protect against and decrease cyberbullying. In Korea, various apps protecting students from harmful media were required to be installed based on the Youth Protection Act. The apps provided by mobile telecommunication companies or the Ministry of Education were introduced and the advantages and disadvantages of such protective apps were explained. This chapter introduces the characteristics, effectiveness, and limitations of the various types of anti-bullying smartphone apps.

"117 Chat" apps: 24-hour school bullying reporting and counseling application ensuring anonymity

The most frequently used application in Korea to prevent school bullying is "117 Chat" developed by Metropolitan Police Agency. The number 117 refers to a hot-line telephone number to report bullying. In Korea, bullying reporting calls which had been distributed to each district or department now has been unified into a single 117 line allowing for efficient management of each report. As the 119 line (911 service in the U.S.) is used for emergencies, the number 117 is strictly used for bullying cases. Compared to using "117 phone line", "117 Chat" allows students to report the case much more easily and rapidly. Currently, "117 Chat" has been distributed throughout

Figure 7.1 Screenshots for “117 Chat” app.

elementary, middle and high schools. This application is free and works on both Android and iOS systems.

Main feature

“117 Chat” can be used by both students and parents. Its main functions can be summarized into three parts, largely: it can report bullying safely through anonymity; it allows direct contact to a professional counselor; and it can provide useful information on bullying. Its core function, however, is that when victims or bystanders report the bullying situation through the application, safely (anonymously), the police officer of that school immediately gets dispatched to cope with the reported situation. Especially, since this report is made via anonymous chatting, it safely protects one’s identity, including, but not limited to, face, voice, and name, thereby relieving any anxiety related to the act of reporting.

Using this application can be described as follows, and Figure 7.1 shows a few important screens captured when you use it.

1. After downloading and installing the application, you can enter your school information after a brief screening process.
2. If you click “Quick counseling” menu, you get connected to a professional counselor in a chat room immediately, and the talk continues in real-time. As shown in the middle of Figure 7.1, you can check the list of available counselors, and you may click one of them on the list to enter the chat room.

3. If you click the "School police officer" menu, you can check your own school police officer and can chat or call the police right away. As shown in the right section of Figure 7.1, you may search the name of the school to check for the school police officer in order to make contact.
4. If you click "117 phone call counseling" on the main screen, you may talk to the bullying specialized counseling service directly on the phone. The 117 phone call counseling service has been provided since 2012, 24 hours a day, 365 days a year. If the reporter wants, in-depth counseling or case investigation are available.
5. If the bullying has been reported or counseling reserved through the above #2, 3, or 4 steps, a) an investigation starts, b) officers will be urgently dispatched, c) the report will be transferred to their school police officer, and d) the report will be transferred to a bullying specialized counseling institution (Wee center, Youth Counseling Welfare center etc.) which will take appropriate measures to follow through and take care of the situation.
6. If you click "School bullying information" menu, related information will be provided so that students or parents will be able to recognize school bullying earlier, for more effective responses. For example, it would provide information such as "How to respond to school bullying".

Characteristics

1) Safe, anonymity-based reporting system: Anonymity minimizes the various limitations and challenges related to expression of one's thought in the offline world (Park and Son, 2016). One of the reasons why victims do not report being bullied to teachers is the fear of being bullied even more severely if it gets revealed that they reported it. Bystanders who witnessed bullying also tend not to report it to teachers because they are anxious about becoming the bullies' next target once their report gets revealed (Hazler, 1996). Therefore, for bystanders who witnessed bullying, if the reporting system allows anonymity, it is more likely for them to report to teachers, thereby suppressing the occurrence of bullying. In fact, since most bullying happens in a situation where bystanders exist (Choi and Nam, 2017; Nam and Hong, 2015; Oh, 2010), if they could report violence anonymously, bullying could be detected more easily (Yun, 2006). Since the majority of bystanders can change their role into defenders who protect victims, most bystanders who witness bullying can stand up for victims, refraining the aggression of bullies.

Using such reporting apps, a sharp increase of reported cases should be expected as in the case of previously implemented system. After the introduction of an anonymous reporting system for sexual discrimination, the number of reports increased by 45% (Ministry of Employment and Labor, 2018). Utilizing such effectiveness, "Red Whistle" – an anonymous reporting system for public officer's corruption – was introduced to more than 100 companies and public institutions, including local government organizations. It not only reports inappropriate behaviors but shows positive effects in providing a great communication channel where members can freely express their opinions within the organization playing the mediator (Yonhap News Agency, 2016, 5–14). An anonymous reporting system also relieves anxiety of victims or bystanders in reporting bullying. Also, for bullies, the more aware they are that "someone might report my bullying actions", the more they refrain from their wrongdoings (Oh and Lee, 2014).

2) Communication with a school police officer, aiding convenience: One of the significant advantages of "117 Chat" is that one may report a bullying case immediately using the chatting application. As more students have access to smartphones, adolescents spend more time on SNS messengers rather than phone calls for communication (Kim and Choi, 2017). Therefore, even though the previous 117 hot-line number exists, messenger communication is preferred. Also, it is possible to send photos via "117 Chat" beyond text-type chatting, so it has the advantage of securing evidence on bullying.

Compared to other anonymous reporting apps, the advantage of "117 Chat" is that it enables direct communication with a school police officer who monitors his or her own school. When one enters "school information", the name and picture of the school police officer for that school appears on the screen, providing the opportunity to start a real-time chat with the police officer. The school police officer system was first introduced in 2012 as a measure to preventing bullying; each police officer manages 10 schools, and is responsible for school bullying and youth behavior.

3) Counseling system which guarantees confidentiality: "117 Chat", besides reporting bullying function, enables counseling with professionals on school bullying issues through a 24-hour chatting system. Most victims tend to have a challenging relationship with friends, showing passive and shy personalities (Kim and Jin, 2019), therefore, it is not easy for such victims to visit a counseling room themselves. Considering their characteristics, they easily feel anxiety in face-to-face conversation environments, so they might comply better in an environment where they can share their honest feelings and thoughts anonymously. Of course, there may be some limitations regarding the effect of counseling because non-verbal communication may not be used compared to face-to-face counseling, but it may relieve psychological stress by providing ways to effectively manage bullying and comfort victims through chat counseling.

They may also switch to phone call counseling by pressing "117 phone call counseling" if they feel limited in text counseling. It is not easy to continue counseling for a long time using a smartphone; its effectiveness may be limited or less than face-to-face counseling. In this case, the counselor may introduce specialized counseling institutions to victims so that they may continue with the sessions. The Metropolitan Police Agency which developed "117 Chat" has established a transfer system using a thorough network with counseling institutions through the Ministry of Education and the Ministry of Gender

Equality and Family, demonstrating its advantage in introducing victims to local counseling institutions.

4) Providing useful information related to school bullying: The final function of "117 Chat" is to provide useful tips related to school bullying to students and their parents. Currently, the provided information includes "7 behavior patterns which children experiencing school violence show" and "How to respond to school bullying in 5 ways?".

["7 behavior patterns which children experiencing school violence show"]

1. They often lose their belongings and ask for a lot of allowances (money);
2. They get alarmed whenever the phone rings; they stay in rooms for receiving calls, and show signs of anxiety all the time;
3. They show aggressive and negative behaviors and word usage;
4. They do not talk to family members and tend to stay in their rooms and use their computer;
5. Their textbooks are often damaged;
6. Their academic scores suddenly drop;
7. They are overly irritated.

["How to respond to school bullying in 5 ways"]

1. Do not ever fight back;
2. First of all, leave the situation;
3. Ask for help from others;
4. Change your commuting route to school; don't be alone;
5. Do not pass by your friends who are getting bullied.

By providing such measures as mentioned above, and suggesting an explanation for each measure, students receive techniques to minimize the damages of being bullied.

Effectiveness and utilization

There has been no study or report suggesting the effectiveness of "117 Chat" directly, but the media reports various cases in which school bullying issues were effectively solved by using "117 Chat". The Gwangju Metropolitan Education Agency is now receiving bullying reports and counseling services through "117 Chat" by connecting "117 Chat" to the bullying counseling service. In Gwangju city, every student and their parents were introduced to this application; once a report is made, nine professional counselors working for the Education Agency providing 24-hour counseling service respond to the incident. The satisfaction was proven to be extremely high (Asia Today News, 2015).

The Ulsan Education Agency and the Metropolitan Police Agency are noted to be successfully decreasing sexual violence – a subtype of school violence through close cooperation with school police officer using "117 Chat". The Police Agency installed a "Sexual Violence Special Unit" to provide a systematic protocol to manage any sexual violence cases in schools. Students as well as teachers may report school violence through "117 Chat". Also, school police officers reported to students, through their actual visits to schools, that any kind of unwanted sexual contact may be reported as "sexual violence". As a result, even if it is a very small positive sign, students are more inclined to ask for counseling, which may prevent an actual sexual crime from taking place. That is, using preventive education on sexual violence and the introduction of "117 Chat" successfully regulated the actual occurrence of sexual violence (The Kyeongnam Ilbo News, 2015).

Comparing the effectiveness of a very similar application called "Mask Chat" which was used in Korea before the introduction of "117 Chat", the effectiveness of "117 Chat" can be predicted. The "Mask Chat" application shows a very similar format to the applications introduced in Chapter 5; being developed privately, each school unit purchases the application to receive anonymous reports on school violence or to provide real-time counseling services. Oh and Lee (2014) carried out a study to prove the effectiveness of the application of "Mask Chat", after designating four elementary, three middle and two high schools as participating groups. They made 2,456 students use "Mask Chat" and compared its effectiveness to other four comparison schools. The frequency of bullying decreased in the participating schools. For students who used "Mask Chat", their confidence in responding to bullying improved. Also, for those students who witnessed the bullying, their intervention behavior also increased: 74.2% of users – students – reported that it was effective because it was convenient (31.9%: it's easy to report the bullying using a cell-phone), because their anonymity was guaranteed (16.3%: since it's impossible to know who reported it, there is no fear of being targeted), because it was helpful in preventing bullying (16.1%: using "Mask Chat" for report may prevent school bullying), and because they can report it immediately (15.1%: it's possible to report via cell-phone right away).

Compared to "Mask Chat", "117 Chat" demonstrates higher effectiveness, providing a unified system in which different reports can be made. Formerly, these calls were distributed by various departments, but now those are managed as a whole in a more comprehensive way. Also, it does not only connect to the police officers but also to the staff working at Wee Centers (counseling centers in school districts) under the Ministry of Education and Youth Counseling Welfare centers under the Ministry of Gender Equality and Family, establishing an effective network. It is unique compared to other anonymous reporting applications in that related departments such as the Police Agency, the Ministry of Education and the Ministry of Gender Equality and Family cooperate together to solve school violence. In other anonymous applications, the school bullying report gets delivered to the teacher or the manager at the school while on "117 Chat", and it reports directly to the school police officer, enhancing the degree of intervention, which, in turn, regulates bullying more effectively. Also, those who receive calls or provide counseling on chat are professionals with experience in solving school bullying cases, and its 24-hour service availability has a strong advantage. Furthermore, another one of its strengths is that it transfers to a more focused service, if necessary, by maintaining a close network to local counseling institutions.

However, "117 Chat" also has some weaknesses. Some pointed out that its follow-up service is somewhat lacking after the victims receive counseling on the chat. Because the counseling service is based on anonymity, it is hard to follow-up on the situation; it is difficult to find out what happened to that particular student. Also, about 260 million KRW (Korean Won) was spent on developing this application, but the average number of users per day utilizing this service was relatively small; they point out that the data to prove its effectiveness based on the investment has been lacking (Yonhap News Agency, 2018). Therefore, the Police Agency has continued to strengthen its function by upgrading "117 Chat" application. As shown in "Mask Chat" earlier, "117 Chat" application should also select several trial schools and trial the Education Agency to secure actual evidence to prove effectiveness in preventing school violence.

"Cyberbullying Vaccine"

"Cyberbullying Vaccine" is an application which the Committee of Victim's Family in School Bullying and "Innocean Worldwide", an advertising agency, developed together: this app provides an opportunity to experience cyberbullying indirectly. The app targeted adults, not adolescents, because its purpose is to let adults be aware of how serious cyberbullying is by them experiencing the cyberbullying youth face. At the final stage of this application, there's an option to sign electronically to promise that users would work hard to stop and prevent cyberbullying. This app assists adults who have learned the seriousness of cyberbullying to become supporters to stop cyberbullying among the youth. It recorded more than 10,000 downloads on Google Playstore; and it's currently used as instruction material at the Police Agency and its outstanding effect have been acknowledged. Unfortunately, it can't be used on iPhones. This app received the Bronze Award at the 2017 Clio Advertising Festival, a renowned festival as one of the "World's Top Three Advertising Festivals", as well as at the Cannes International Advertising Festival and New York Festival, the all-time dream for everyone working in the advertising industry. Also, it received a Special Award for new-type advertising sector at 2017 Korea's Advertising Awards.

Main feature of the app

Virtual Experience contents provided in this app are based on actual cases. It includes some cursing and sensitive pictures, so you can only enter the app

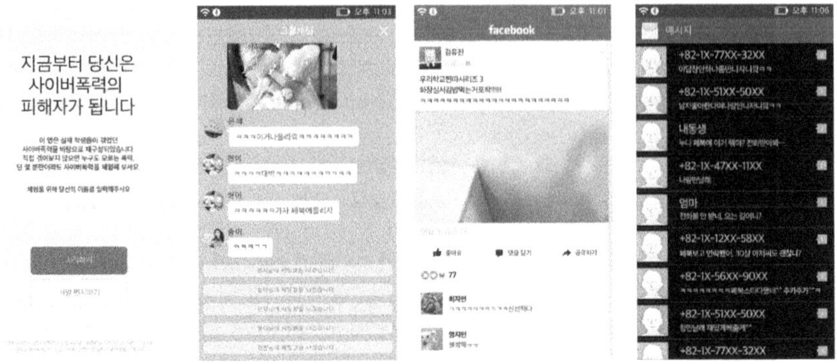

Entering your name | Kakao Talk bullying | Facebook bullying | Text message bullying

Figure 7.2 Screenshots for "Cyberbullying Vaccine" app.

with adult verification. You can understand the seriousness of school bullying through experiencing victims' emotions and fear semi-directly by becoming the victims of "cyberbullying". Directions to use this application are explained here: screenshots of the main screens shown in this application are as follows. According to the LIME (Level of Immersion in Media Experience) model, this app is based on level 2 (Avatar mode) or level 3 (Actor mode). When a player launches the app, they enter his or her name. Therefore, it is very easy to immerse the player into the characters in the game. The player is under the illusion that he or she is being perpetrated. Therefore, it is close to level 3. But the story of the game is not his or her own story. The players feel like they are being attacked, but it's actually the way they project themselves on other people's stories. Therefore, the experience of this game can be seen as a semi-direct experience of violence, so it is close to level 2 as well.

1. After completing the adult verification, users play a phone call from a fake bully named "Minji". Most users are surprised by this because the screen shows an incoming call and they can hear the phone ringing. Once they receive the call, they hear a threatening voice saying "Hey! Are you kidding me? What took you so long to take the call?"
2. Then, as shown in the first picture (Figure 7.2), brief information about the application appears on the screen. Users are recommended to enter their real names for an even more realistic experience; once they press the "Start" button, the "cyberbullying" begins. Since the bullying starts with their name, it appears extremely realistic.
3. Notifications come up continuously on Kakao Talk message. Once you open the Kakao Talk application, a group chatroom pops up and the

bullying starts as the bullies begin saying harsh words and curses. All five friends continue to send "text bombs" of hideous words as they also include "humiliating" pictures in the mix. A series of cursing, humiliations and insults are sent, after which the five bullies leave the chatroom all at once (see the second picture in Figure 7.2).

4 After they leave the Kakao Talk chatroom, the notifications continue to pop up as it notifies you that someone is posting on Facebook. Once you start Facebook, you can see the posts where bullies continue to make fun of you. You are able to see that the bullies are posting photos and videos of you getting bullied. If you play the posted video, you can see the "humiliating video". Besides that, five other pictures and bullying posts appear as they fill up your wall (third picture of Figure 7.2).

5. When you close the Facebook app, you hear notifications telling you that you have just received texts. Once you open up the message application, you can see the messages from your mother and sister as well as 15 texts of cursing and insults. You can touch each text to read; all of them are messages containing a varying mixture of insults, threats and curses. The message from your sibling says "What's up with your Facebook? Please answer the call" (fourth picture on Figure 7.2).

6. Once you experience firsthand all three types of cyberbullying – Kakao Talk, Facebook, texts, the phrase that raises awareness of the dangers of cyberbullying is presented by quoting a cyberbullying victim's suicide note (part of last will of cyberbullying victims) A statement appears saying "Children cannot escape this nightmare on their own. They require your help and your care, right now". Then, the buttons for "signature" and "Go to counseling" appear. If you click the "Signature" button, you can sign electronically that you would work hard to prevent cyberbullying from now on, while the "Go to counseling" button takes you to the counseling page – the bulletin board for the committee of families of victims.

Main characteristics

1) Utilization of virtual experience: The biggest feature of this application is that users indirectly experience cyberbullying by applying the principle of virtual reality. Through this virtual reality method, users enter three actual types of bullying. Also, the interactions within the application make the experience even more realistic – playing videos posted on Facebook or checking their inbox by touching them. The advantages of such virtual reality are immersion and reality, where immersion refers to the degree of being immersed into a certain experience, and reality refers to a phenomenon where one feels like being in virtual reality; users feel being cyberbullied while activating this application.

In fact, many comments from users are posted on YouTube. Comments below are excerpts from actual users of this application.

(speechless, shocked at horrible results for victims)

I virtually experienced cyberbullying for 7 minutes and 35 seconds, and I think it would be so difficult to endure such bullying. Even if I had had a strong mental fortitude, if I were to experience such an attack continuously, I wouldn't be able to hold up. No matter what, it became more and more severe. And I think we need to provide solutions and all of us need to work hard so students don't experience something like this ever again.

(Male student, participant)

Honestly, I was indifferent towards cyberbullying. But after this experience, I am now willing go out of my way and stop those bullies if I were to meet any in the future. This game allowed me to relate on an emotional level, and I could imagine how painful these experiences must have been to be victims, and how serious this is as I experienced myself becoming "Wang-ta". I hope many people would acknowledge how serious cyberbullying is through this application.

(Female student, participant)

2) Experiencing three types of bullying: Through this app, users get to experience three types of cyberbullying – Kakao Talk messenger in the form of a group chat, Facebook SNS bulletin board that is open to everyone, and text messages shared exclusively to one person. These three types of bullying are the most common when it comes to cyberbullying in Korea. According to the 2014 survey by the Youth Violence Prevention Foundation, Kakao Talk showed the highest record of 41.6% while SNS such as Facebook or Kakaostory followed with 34.5% (Youth Violence Prevention Foundation, 2015). Especially, the most frequent case is bullying using Kakao Talk messenger application, called "Ka-ta". This term is now registered in the Korean Dictionary as it's extremely commonly used; "Ka-ta" is defined as a "slang to indicate Wang-ta at Kakao Talk or Kakaostory used among teenagers". Kakao Talk is an instant messenger application that was started back in 2010, and is currently the most widely used app in Korea with over 94.4% of the population using this application on a daily basis. On this app, victims are forcefully invited to the group talks (chatroom), and they get bullied by receiving a tremendous volume of chats that typically include cursing and insults, or otherwise commonly known as "Ka-ta". After being satisfied with their bullying, the bullies leave the chatroom at the same time, leaving the victim all alone. This is known as the "Room Bombing" type.

On the other hand, bullying through Facebook spreads quite rapidly because the degree of publicity is wider than the group chat room. After surveying the platform for cyberbullying in England, unlike in Korea, Facebook showed the highest record of 52%, while MSN followed with 24% (Beatbullying, 2012). Since the number of Facebook user is always increasing, it is plausible to see the increase of cyberbullying cases on this platform in the future.

Finally, text messages are only done in one-on-one situations; it's mostly used when bullies do not want to reveal their identity. Oh and Li (2019) studied the biggest psychological shock in these three types of bullying, confirming that the biggest change in emotions was when they experienced cyberbullying on Facebook. It is understood that victims are most concerned when their humiliating posts can be seen by the general public.

Effectiveness

Oh and Li (2019) measured changes in the psychological characteristics of 232 randomly selected female college students after their experiences of "Cyberbullying Vaccine". First, they were to watch the video demonstrating the "Cyberbullying Vaccine" application and compare the degree of positive and negative emotions before and after the video. Positive and negative emotions were measured on a 5-point Likert scale using PANAS (Positive and Negative Affect Schedule), which consists of 10 questions, created by Watson, Clark, and Tellegen (1988). After measuring their average time of phone use, frequently used features on the phone, and typical emotional mood, they were measured again after watching the "Cyberbullying Vaccine" application video. While experiencing the application, they were indirectly experiencing three different cyberbullying methods – Kakao Talk, Facebook, and text messages – then their personal psychological conditions were measured. In order to compare the difference of positive/negative emotions before and after watching the video, a paired t-test was carried out. The results showed a significant difference. As can be seen in Figure 7.3, the positive emotions sharply decrease while the negative emotions increased. The positive emotion decreased from 12.27 to 4.34 (64.6%) and the negative increased from 11.28 to 18.40 (63.1%). There are not many experimental studies on victims of cyberbullying, and victims being cyberbullied are known to experience negative emotions such as anxiety, depression, and trauma (Jeong, 2015). Even though this study gives an indirect experience rather than the actual one, such change in emotions was shown to be extremely significant.

Legalization of installing youth protection application

In Korea, it became mandatory for mobile telecommunication companies to provide measures to screen out any harmful content or illegal pornography when signing contracts with youth mobile users from April 2015. It is a protective measure to safeguard our youth from the many harmful contents on the Internet. Therefore, electronic communication business owners now must provide screening measures to prohibit any intake of harmful information on the Internet according to the Youth Protective Act and the Act on Promotion of Information and Communications Network Utilization and Information Protection when adolescents purchase cell phones. Youth

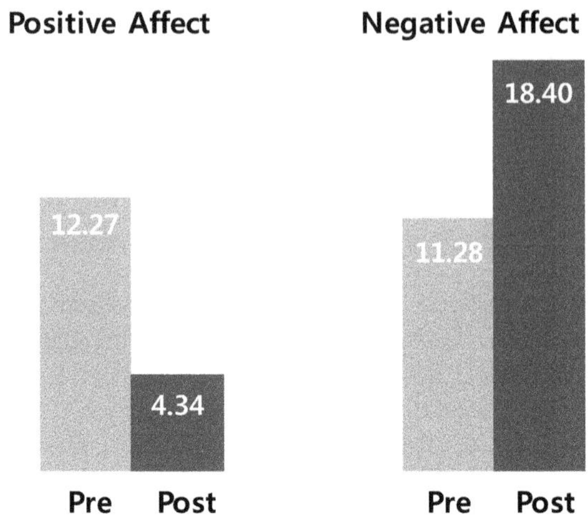

Figure 7.3 Difference of positive/negative emotions before and after cyberbullying virtual experience.

smartphone users must install at least one of the screening applications. Currently, major mobile telecommunication companies provide filtering services to screen out any harmful websites or information through its filtering application. When the youth opens up his or her own smartphone, filtering measures and contents should be explained to the youth and legal caregivers. Also, it should be confirmed whether the filtering measure was successfully installed. Furthermore, if the filtering measure was deleted or has not been activated for longer than 15 days, it should be notified to legal caregivers on a monthly basis.

According to this Act, every mobile telecommunication company now provides such protective apps: the "T Youth Safety Package" among these demonstrates the feature of monitoring by parents related to bullying. The "T Youth Safety Package" provides eight different protective features as one unified application, as shown below.

1. Alert for any sign of school bullying;
2. Controlling time for smartphone usage;
3. Looking up history of smartphone usage;
4. Alert for "concern or issue" search;
5. Searching children's location;
6. "117 Chat" counseling for school bullying (Police Agency);
7. Auto-screening of harmful sites and contents;
8. Safety control including preventing usage during walking or cell-phone payment.

For instance, "Alert for any sign of school bullying" monitors any suspicious texts among SNS, mobile messages and texts a child receives, sending the history of received messages to their caregivers' smartphone. Smartphone usage time and the history monitoring feature assists children to keep track of their usage pattern so that they can prevent smartphone addiction and manage their use by setting an adequate and healthy time schedule. Also, for their own safety, the feature guarantees the children's safety by stopping the cell-phone from functioning if they use the phone while walking. It also works to screen out any harmful website contents. Another feature connects to the reporting app, "117 Chat".

Apart from the protective apps provided by telecommunication companies, the Ministry of Education launched "Safe School Life" in 2015, assisting in the safety of students, and provided the safety manual to every school at the same time. It consists of 55 safety-related materials on eight different areas in and out of school life, including school bullying and group bullies. As shown in Figure 7.4 below, it provides information on how to report when one witnesses school bullying. Also, it gives a quiz to clear misunderstanding on group bullying. Furthermore, it provides information on how to seek help related to bullying from the Ministry of Education, Police Agency, Youth Violence Prevention Foundation and Wee Centers in the country.

Since it became mandatory to install youth protective application, various applications have been developed and are being used besides the apps introduced above. Such apps can be utilized as effective measures when

Figure 7.4 Screenshots for "Safe School Life" app.

bullying occurs and prevent cyberbullying in advance. However, such apps also have their limitations. For example, Korea Communications Commissions developed and shared the "Smart Safety Dream" app in 2015 aiming to protect the youth from the harmful online environment. However, the number of users kept decreasing year after year; in 2017, the download count was less than 2,000. Once the app is installed on the children's smartphone, it detects violence-suspicious texts and monitors what the children search on the Internet. Parents can verify the website which their children looked up on the Internet. Even though the app can only be installed under the mutual agreement between children and parents, it has raised concerns that it violates the privacy of children since it records what the kids search online (Digital Daily, 2018). Before installing, parents should spend time talking to their kids and make them understand the importance of the app. However, in cases where the app is installed forcefully, it can worsen the relationship between parents and their children. Adolescence is a time when children get psychologically independent from parents, and increase their autonomy. Therefore, it is perfectly normal for children to resist the usage of such protective apps. In fact, it is understandable that the customer rating for youth protective apps is quite low. Most users who complete the evaluation are the children who use this protective app, expressing their complaints to the developers through completing the rating.

To use various the applications studied above, it is necessary to consider the following for more effective utilization:

- For anonymous reporting apps to identify bullying, it has its advantage of convenience in reporting. However, it's possible that people may use it for fun (as a joke), and that it may not be able to identify the actual victim immediately on a very urgent report.
- For anonymous reporting apps, its effectiveness is yet to be confirmed. Even though the user satisfaction is quite high, it seems that further study is necessary. Their actual effectiveness can be determined by comparing schools using these apps and control schools.
- The counseling feature of "117 Chat" is very strong because it is available 24 hours a day, 365 days a year. However, to provide such service, it requires a considerable amount of budget and staff. Therefore, in order to utilize it, it requires close cooperation among related departments (Police Agency, Ministry of Education, Ministry of Gender Equality and Family, etc.).
- Virtual-reality-based applications show great promise in the educational field as they give students the opportunity to experience the severity of cyberbullying indirectly. On the contrary, students who may have experienced similar cases might feel discomfort. Some might learn various ways to bully others. Such risks should be considered in advance.
- Mandatory installation of protective applications on phones are effective in protecting young kids from the many hazards that exist online.

However, beyond screening out the harmful information, the apps does allow parents to look up the history of their kids' smartphone usage which may worsen the relationship between the child and the parent.

References

Asia Today News. (2015, July 2). *Gwangju Metropolitan Office of Education, Korea's No. 1 in Terms of Satisfaction with Eradicating School Violence.* Retrieved from www.asiatoday.co.kr/view.php?key=20150702010000911

Beatbullying. (2012). *Virtual Violence II: Progress and Challenges in the Fight Against Cyberbullying.* London: Beatbullying.

Choi, Z. H. and Nam, Y. O. (2017). A study on school violence and bystanders' role. *The Journal of Welfare and Counselling Education*, *6*(2), 275–297. doi:10.20497/jwce.2017.6.2.275

Digital Daily. (2018, October, 14). *Will "Smart Safety Dream" App of the Korea Communications Commission Continue Its Business Even If Users Turn Away From It?* Retrieved from www.ddaily.co.kr/news/article/?no=173600

Hazler, R. J. (1996). *Breaking the Cycle of Violence: Interventions for Bullying and Victimization.* Washington, DC: Accelerated Development.

Jeong, M. K. (2015). The mediating effects of social competence and perceived social support on the relationship between cyberbullied experience in adolescents and social anxiety. *Korean Journal of Counseling*, *16*(2), 195–211. doi:10.15703/kjc.16.2.201504.195

Kim, K. E. and Choi, E. H. (2017). The relationship between school-violence victimization and cyber-violence behavior in youth: The mediating effect of cyber-violence victimization. *Journal of School Social Work*, *38*, 75–97. doi:10.20993/jssw.38.4

Kim, M. R. and Jin, M. K. (2019). The effects of the Gestalt Relationship Improvement Program (GRIP) on interpersonal anxiety and peer relationships amongst elementary school students experiencing school violence. *Korean Journal of Play Therapy*, *22*(1), 81–103. doi:10.17641/kapt.22.1.5

Ministry of Employment and Labor. (2018, September 6). *Report on the Operation of an Anonymous Reporting Center for Sexual Discrimination in Employment.* Retrieved from www.moel.go.kr/news/enews/report/enewsView.do?news_seq=9158

Nam, M. A. and Hong, B. S. (2015). A study of factors affecting the bystander's role in school violence. *Journal of the Korean Society of Child Welfare*, *50*, 109–144.

Oh, I. (2010). Psychological factors influencing bystanders' behavioral reactions to bullying: A focus on empathy and aggression. *The Journal of Elementary Education*, *23*(1), 45–63.

Oh, I. and Lee, S-Y. (2014, August). Effectiveness and utilization of Mask Chat app for preventing school violence. *2014 Annual Conference of Korea Counseling Association.* Seoul.

Oh, I. and Li, M. (2019, June). Relations of emotional self-regulation, negative affect, anger and aggression among provocative victims to cyberbullying. *2019 Annual Conference of Korean Education Research Association.* Seoul.

Park, D. S. and Son, E. J. (2016). Factors influencing cyberbullying behavior: Anonymity, aggression, and attitudes toward cyberbullying. *Korean Journal of Counseling*, *17*(4), 313–331. doi:10.15703/kjc.17.4.201608.313

The Kyeongnam Ilbo News. (2015, October 13). *We Need to Protect Students from Sex Offenders*. Retrieved from www.gnnews.co.kr/news/articleView.html?idxno=252482

Watson, D., Clark, L. A., and Tellegen, A. (1988). Development and validation of the brief measures of positive and negative affect: The PANAS scales. *Journal of Personality and Social Psychology*, *54*(6), 1063–1070. doi:10.1037/0022-3514.54.6.1063

Yonhap News Agency. (2016, May 14). *The Effect of the Anonymous Reporting System on Public Official Corruption in Gangwon Province: From 0 cases in 5 years to 8 cases in 1 year*. Retrieved from www.yna.co.kr/view/AKR20160513152400062

Yonhap News Agency. (2018, October 3). *The Effectiveness of Six Police Apps, Which Cost 1.3 Billion Won, Is Questionable and "No Visitor Count"*. Retrieved from www.yna.co.kr/view/AKR20181003033500004?input=1195m

Youth Violence Prevention Foundation (2015). *Annual National School Violence Survey Result*. Seoul, Korea: Youth Violence Prevention Foundation.

Yun, H. J. (2006). Perceived anonymity in an online social support community: A hierarchical structure of the concept and its effects on online public disclosure. *Korean Journal of Journalism & Communication Studies*, *50*(6), 305–332.

8 Challenging moral disengagement caused by anonymity

Japanese preventive practices

Tomoyuki Kanetsuna and Kazuhiko Ishihara

Beliefs about anonymity on the Internet and their effects on online deviant behavior

As discussed in Chapter 2, the current situation of cyberbullying and other Internet-related problems among children and youth in Japan is somewhat problematic. Children are engaging in various risky behaviors including excessive use to the point of dependency on mobile devices and online activities, inappropriate posting to various social networking services (SNS), using abusive language, and accessing sexual and violent materials. One of the factors responsible for these deviant online behaviors is commonly held beliefs about anonymity on the Internet. In this chapter, we will cover this issue as well as safe Internet use practices.

Use of social media such as bulletin board systems, weblogs, and various kinds of SNS has rapidly increased during the last decade, including among children and adolescents. Further, among social media users in Japan, about 70% reported a preference for anonymous communication (Internet White Paper, 2008). Orita (2009), however, claimed that the idea of anonymity on the Internet is a false belief, as it is technologically possible for site administrators or Internet service providers to identify by whom, when, and where a particular comment was posted. However, among end users without expertise, because it appears possible for them to communicate without revealing their identities, it is generally assumed that they can be anonymous in cyberspace. In fact, one of the reasons for inappropriate or aggressive online behavior is this commonly held belief about anonymity. The Japanese National Police Agency (2012) reported that about 74% of those arrested for illegal online acts committed them because of the belief that they would not be identified and, therefore, caught.

Takeuchi, Toda, and Takahashi (2015) argued that strong beliefs about anonymity on the Internet could lead to "moral disengagement." Moral disengagement, originally theorized by Bandura (1999), is the process of convincing oneself of being exempt from moral standards in a particular context by separating moral reactions from inhumane conduct and by disabling the mechanism of self-sanction. This state could trigger the possibility of people easily becoming perpetrators in the online environment. The Japanese Ministry of Education, Culture, Sports, Science and Technology (MEXT) (2008a), in the "Manual for Dealing with Cyberbullying" ("*Net joh no ijime ni kansuru taiou manyuaru*"), warned schools and teachers that anonymous communication on the Internet increases the likelihood of children's involvement in cyberbullying and other Internet-mediated problematic behaviors as both perpetrators and victims.

Strong beliefs about anonymity on the Internet have been found not only to promote online perpetration and deviant behaviors, but also have negative effects on victims. Aoyama, Saxon, and Fearon (2010) pointed out that it is difficult for victims of cyberbullying to seek help because of the anonymity of the perpetrators. They argued that because perpetrators of cyberbullying can remain anonymous, the victims cannot identify who the bullies are in the first place. Furthermore, when hurtful gossip and rumors are spread on SNS, it is highly possible that the entire class or even the whole school is witness to the harassment, making it even harder for the victim to seek help from peers (Aoyama, Saxon, and Fearon, 2010). Ono and Saito (2008) noted that owing to the anonymity afforded by the Internet, victims of cyberbullying often cannot identify who attacked them, and become highly suspicious, even with their close friends. In its survey of 13,605 junior high school students and 5,724 high school students, the Saitama Prefectural Board of Education (2009) revealed that while about half of the participants reported that perpetrators of cyberbullying were "classmates" or "higher-year students," the other half stated that the perpetrators were "anonymous people." In his self-report questionnaire study, Kanetsuna (2016) examined the effects of beliefs regarding anonymity on children's risk perception, anxiety regarding online victimization, and prevention-related awareness. As per the results, those who had stronger beliefs about anonymity showed lower levels of risk perception and anxiety regarding victimization, which led to lower levels of prevention-related awareness. Kanetsuna claimed that owing to strong beliefs about anonymity, the Internet environment is conducive to bullying by promoting perpetration on one side and weakening risk perception and awareness on the other.

Morio and Buchholz (2009) used a three-step hierarchy to explain the concept of online anonymity. The first step, which is the lowest and most basic, is termed "visual anonymity," where you cannot visually identify the person you communicate with. The second step is the "dissociation of real and online identities," where it is possible to distinguish a particular person online through their username but off-line identification is not possible. The highest level is the "lack of identifiability," where a person is unidentifiable both online and off-line.

A free communication app such as LINE, which is one of the major environments for cyberbullying among Japanese children today, can be considered representative of visual anonymity. Here, while children are usually aware of who they are communicating with, they cannot physically confirm the person's identity. In such a state of visual anonymity, there are three potential consequences. The first is that you cannot be sure if the person you are communicating with is, in fact, the person you were expecting. This relates to the problem of "spoofing." For example, someone intentionally makes inappropriate posts to SNS or makes homepage with inappropriate contents using your username. In another example, a stranger may approach you pretending to be your classmate. In the first case, people online cannot be sure if the comment was posted by you or someone pretending to be you. Similarly, in the second case, you cannot be sure if the person is someone you know or a complete stranger. This suggests the danger of trusting others easily in the Internet environment.

The second consequence of visual anonymity is the lack of non-verbal information during communication. When you cannot see the person's facial expressions and gestures or hear the person's voice, it can be very difficult to accurately interpret their emotional state or true meaning. This leads to misunderstandings between the writers and readers of messages, which could be one of the causes of cyberbullying. Sproull and Kiesler (1986) argued that this lack of non-verbal information weakens the sense of the other person's social existence, in turn, weakening the behavioral suppression that usually exists in a face-to-face situation. Kiesler, Siegel, and McGuire (1984) referred to this as "social anonymity" and, in the context of the deindividuation effect, argued that because of the dominance of the social identity, individual responsibility within the group becomes vague.

The last consequence of visual anonymity is the lack of social impact (Latané, 1981). As per Latané, social impact is the degree of influence people are affected by others. The strength of the impact varies depending on the social status of the person you communicate with, the physical distance between persons, and the number of people you are communicating with. In the state of visual anonymity, the person you are communicating with is invisible, making the impact of spatial closeness with the person very small. If the level of anonymity is higher, and you are unaware of the person's age or social status, for instance, the impact will be even smaller. This small social impact may reduce the tension between persons, leading, in turn, to a lack of consideration and care for the other person.

In addition to these psychological consequences of visual anonymity, Pornari and Wood (2010) argued that because perpetrators do not directly see the damage caused by their actions, cyberbullying often escalates easily. As they are not witness to the victim's hurt or depression, it is difficult for the perpetrators to experience empathy/sympathy toward the victim or shame/guilt regarding their actions.

In summary, in order to protect children from being involved in risky online situations, it is essential to provide appropriate information about how the Internet works so that they can gage the potential consequences of their actions before doing something inappropriate online. In particular, it is important to effectively explain to them that despite appearances, they can never be truly anonymous online. Therefore, they should beware that the false beliefs about anonymity on the Internet could enable cyberbullying and inappropriate online behaviors as well as vulnerability to victimization.

Tackling cyberbullying and so on by using online apps and teaching materials

Against this backdrop, the MEXT made an appeal to emphasize information morals education in their courses-of-study for primary and junior high schools in 2008 and again in 2017. As per the MEXT, it is essential for children to acquire information utilization skills including adequate information literacy and morals, which form the basis of general learning and help prevent various Internet-related problems (MEXT, 2008b, 2017a). Asada and Hara (2017) examined the effectiveness of annual whole-school meetings for raising cyberbullying prevention awareness. Although the meetings were held twice a year over the course of three years, the effect seemed fairly limited to some types of cyberbullying. Awareness-raising activities for cyberbullying prevention are certainly important, but they should form a part of children's daily activities.

Indeed, according to the latest national survey, about 77%, 93%, and 96% of primary, junior high, and high school children, respectively, reported having had opportunities to learn about the risks and dangers of the online environment, and most reported having acquired this information at school. As for the contents of such education, risks of online communication was found to be the most frequently covered topic (75%) followed by privacy protection (61%), child pornography (48%), and Internet addiction (44%) (Japanese Cabinet Office, 2019).

In light of the abovementioned information, various teaching and self-learning apps and materials for information literacy and morals have been developed in Japan. These can be classified into four categories by two axes. The first axis is learning style, where one end is conventional mass learning and the other is individualized learning. The second axis is children's experiences, where one end is passive and instructional and the other is active and experiential. Figure 8.1 shows the cross-model that applies children's learning situation to the types of these two axes. The "traditional classroom instruction" is a passive and instructional learning experience in a traditional mass learning situation. The "classroom active learning" is also set in the traditional mass learning situation but gives more active and experiential learning experience. Finally, the "individual/networked active learning" is an active and experiential learning experience in an individualized learning situation. Although this figure does not describe the materials apply to passive instructional experience in the individualized learning situation, it is assumed when children use materials of "traditional classroom instruction" alone at home.

In relation to above categorization, Ieshima (2019) proposed the "Level of Immersion in Multimedia Experience" (LIME) model to explain the immersion produced by varying levels of multimedia experiences (see

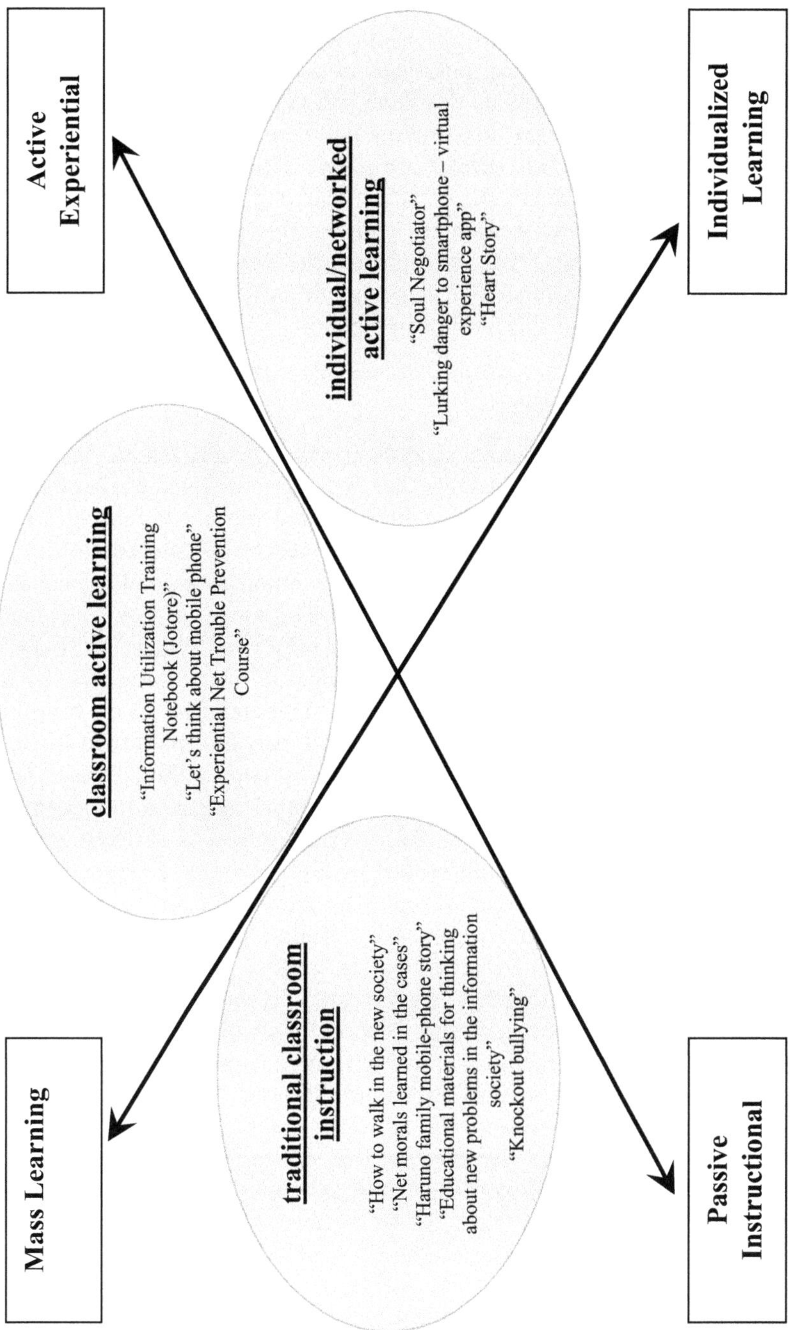

Figure 8.1 Cross-model of learning situation.

Chapter 3 for details). If you think about various online experiences with reference to this model, just viewing someone's posts on SNS, for example, will be an audience-level experience that produces only a surface level of immersion. In the cross-model described above, the traditional classroom instruction can be considered as this level. However, if you yourself engage in something on the Internet, like posting comments or pictures, using your avatar, this can be a slightly deeper immersive experience. In terms of the cross-model, much of the classroom active learning is at this level. Further, if you act online as if you were in the real world without your avatar, as in the case of virtual reality, this can produce the deepest immersive experience. Some of the classroom active learning and individual/networked active learning can be seen as at this level of immersion.

Traditional classroom instruction

The teaching style in Japanese schools is traditionally "mass learning," wherein 30 to 40 students gather together in a classroom and share common learning materials. The information literacy and morals taught in school are no exception. Most teachers use common teaching materials to discuss problems related to Internet use and online communication, and to help children develop an appropriate mindset and sound judgment. A typical teaching material used in such a traditional mass learning environment is "How to walk in the net society (*Net shakai no arukikata*)" (Japan Association for Promotion of Education Technology, 2019). This material has a long history and has been updated several times since it was first published in 2000. Essentially, it comprises Flash animation video clips telling short stories wherein the characters get in some sort of trouble owing to inappropriate Internet use. The aim is to improve children's awareness of various risk situations on the Internet. It takes about five minutes to watch a single clip, and children are required to consider why such an incident occurred, and how to solve the problem if they themselves face a similar situation. The storylines serve to warn viewers of the risks of online trading, Internet auctions, and online communication, together with copyright infringement, excessive gaming and Internet use, online fraud, cyberbullying, online criminals, and so on. There are many other similar teaching materials presenting short stories on various kinds of unsavory incidents on the Internet. "Net Morals Learned in the Cases" ("*Jirei de manabu Net moraru*") published by the Hiroshima Textbook Sales (Hiroshima Kyohan, 2019) is subject to fees, but in addition to video materials, includes worksheets for children, teaching guidance, and materials for parents too. In 2009, NTT Docomo, one of the biggest mobile providers in Japan, released "Haruno family mobile-phone story" ("*Harunoke keitai monogatari*") as part of its corporate social responsibility (CSR) (NTT Docomo, 2009). This is again a teaching material for online morals including a set of video materials, teaching guidance, and worksheets. In 2017, the MEXT published the videos of 51 live-action dramas on YouTube as "Educational materials for thinking about new problems in the information society" (MEXT, 2017b). These materials are supposed to be used by teachers during lessons, but of course children can independently use them to review previous classes and acquire new knowledge about online literacy and morals. Accordingly, apps can also be considered as examples of the audience mode at the individual level.

Class-wide multi-level learning

The teaching materials introduced above are basically passive and instructional, developed for use in traditional mass learning. Furthermore, in the context of the LIME model, they can all be categorized as the "audience" mode of experience, where the level of immersion can be fairly limited, making it difficult for many children to relate to the events they see in the videos. However, there are also apps and materials meant for more active and experiential types of classes, where children have access to more immersive experiences. One such app is the "Information utilization training notebook" ("*Jouho katsuyo toreiningu noto/Jotore*") (Bunkeido, 2014). By allotting each student one computer terminal and allowing them to use it during the class, there is more scope for experience despite the fact that it is still mass learning. As discussed above, many children today have their own mobile devices and practically unrestricted access to the Internet; therefore, it is relatively easy for them to get involved in risky situations. In such a context, it is not enough for teachers to take the lead and discuss problematic cases while children passively listen. Instead, in the safe confines of the classroom, it is important for children to understand the characteristics of the Internet and online communication. This can help them gain awareness regarding potential problems and hopefully acquire the practical ability to solve them. The *Jotore*, which has been developed based on such principles, includes five contents, each of which has its own theme such as "character input," "online searching," "copyright," "online morals," and "online safety." One of the features of the *Jotore* is its coverage of the three modes of the LIME model. For example, it utilizes manga and animation for the purposes of instruction and explanation, making it appealing to children as they view these contents in audience mode. In the "online morals" section, however, children experience online chatting with their classmates, which falls in the avatar mode of multimedia experience. One of the rubrical characteristics of this material is found in this section, where children are given a chance to experience anonymous online chatting with other classmates by using pre-decided nicknames and avatars. The key to this section is that teachers can change children's anonymous nicknames to their real names at any point during the chat. Can you imagine what happens when children realize they are no longer anonymous? While it may have its pros and cons, the goal is to teach children the danger of having false beliefs about anonymity on the Internet by showing them that it is possible to identify who wrote a particular post even if it was originally written anonymously. Since this practice is a deeper immersive experience incorporating avatars, it is much more personal than just watching videos from a third-party perspective.

Mito (2017) introduced the class-based cyberbullying prevention program for junior high school students. This program combines several apps and teaching materials, covering all three modes of the LIME model. Each app and material is to be used for different purposes. For example, a simulation game app called "Soul Negotiator" (GREE) and a teaching material called "Let's think about mobile phones" ("*Minnade kangaeyou ke-tai/suma-tofon*") (Softbank) are both used for learning about and contemplating ways to reduce cyberbullying. An audiovisual material called "Knockout bullying" ("*ijime wo nokku auto*") (NHK) is used to help develop the courage to intervene and help others who are being attacked on the Internet. The program aims to change the attitude toward cyberbullying from that of a passive outsider ("it's nothing to do with me") to an active defender ("I must do something about it") by giving children opportunities to exchange opinions and think about what they can and should do about the situation together. By doing this, they can understand the importance of taking small steps to save other people and simultaneously understand what is involved in taking such small steps.

Individual/class-wide active learning

Similar actions have been carried out by the Kyoto Prefectural Police Department, which, ahead of the whole country, developed a learning app commissioned to a private IT company with the Kyoto Prefectural Consumer Safety Center. Users of this app can virtually experience four types of online risk situations: 1) inappropriate posting to SNS, 2) trouble with nasty emails and messages, 3) click fraud, and 4) fake site fraud. While the app is designed for users to learn about real-world online risks, it is also an interactive educational tool for children. This virtual experience app is also used to conduct the "Experiential Net Trouble Prevention Course" for children (Kyoto Prefectural Police Department, 2019).

Individual/networked active learning

The teaching materials and apps for online literacy and morals introduced above are designed for use mainly in mass learning situations. However, there are some apps, such as "Lurking danger to smartphone: Virtual experience application" ("*sumaho ni hisomu kiken – gijitaiken apuri*") (Digital Arts) and "Heart Story" ("*Kokoro Sutorii*") (Tokyo Metropolitan Board of Education), that have been developed for more personal use. Both are smartphone apps aimed at educating children and raising awareness about online risks through stories about Internet-mediated problems including cyberbullying, trouble with peers, overuse of smartphones, and disclosure of personal information. These are very similar to the teaching materials introduced so far in their concepts and aims but are meant for more personal use. Besides the development of apps for personal use, Digital Arts also engages in various CSR activities, including Internet security education and providing free educational materials for children, parents, and educators. "Heart Story" is one of the apps developed by a local board of education (Tokyo), and there are several other local governments that have developed similar apps and teaching materials.

In addition to such practices, some apps have been developed for the purpose of reporting online problems. "Kids' Sign" (School Guardian, 2013) and "STOPit" (STOPit Japan, 2018) are smartphone apps aiming to prevent and intervene in bullying and Internet-mediated problems but utilizing different approaches. Both apps are designed to allow victims and bystanders of cyberbullying and other malicious online behavior to consult or report the incidents anonymously. These apps focus more on intervening in ongoing bullying and perpetration by providing children with a safe environment for seeking help. This is particularly useful for children in Japan who often find it difficult to seek help when they are victimized and for teachers who often struggle to identify bullying situations because of children's reluctance to report them (Kanetsuna, Smith, and Morita, 2006). The great thing about these apps is that they are making positive use of the anonymity of the Internet. Previously, the negative aspects of anonymity, such as promoting bullying and lowering awareness of prevention, have often been given attention, but these apps encourage victims and bystanders, who would otherwise hesitate to seek help owing to fear of retaliation from the perpetrators, to report incidents. Therefore, once a case is reported on these apps, it is of the utmost importance for the concerned authorities to take immediate action, or people will be dissuaded from using these apps again. Now, other similar approaches are beginning to take root. One of these is using existing SNS such as LINE for anonymous consultation and reporting. An advantage of using existing apps is the ease of inviting children as they already use them. While children have to be encouraged to install apps such as "Kids' Sign" and "STOPit" on their smartphones, the use of existing apps simplifies the procedure.

So far, we have introduced some of the major apps and teaching materials developed for preventing cyberbullying and Internet-mediated problems. However, it is important to keep in mind that none of these can prevent bullying and online risks on their own. Instead, the intention behind the development of all these apps and materials has been to raise awareness. As many children today possess their own mobile devices, it is difficult for adults to monitor their actions. Therefore, when children are faced with risk situations, adults most often do not even know about it. Thus, it is essential for children to learn about risk situations, develop preventive mindsets, and independently work toward keeping themselves safe. Of course, schools and teachers must continue to monitor what children are doing with their devices and provide appropriate information in line with actual risk situations. The important question is not which apps to use but how to make maximal use of these apps to protect children from various online risk situations.

Effectiveness of prevention/intervention by using apps and teaching materials

The effectiveness of these apps and teaching materials has not yet been systematically evaluated, and there could be variations depending on how and in what circumstances they are used. However, there are positive reports about some apps.

"STOPit," the anonymous help-seeking app, was developed in the US in 2014. Since then, about 6,000 schools in the US have implemented the program, and there have been more than three million downloads (STOPit Japan). In Japan, the city of Kashiwa in Chiba prefecture decided to introduce the app to state junior high schools in 2018, and it has since been reported that 486 of the approximately one million eligible junior high school students in Kashiwa city are registered on the app (Kashiwa City, 2019; *Mainichi News Paper*, 2019). Furthermore, the number of consultations for bullying has increased rapidly to 133, about five times the consultations by telephone and email in the previous year. It has also been reported that about 40% of these reported cases were related to bullying and Internet-mediated troubles (*Mainichi News Paper*, 2019). Kashiwa city positively evaluated the effectiveness of the app by saying: "we can be ready to deal with bullying before it becomes serious," and pointed out as a background factor its success that mobile apps are among the most popular communication tools for children. Similarly, "STOPit" was implemented in a high school in Bizen city and a secondary school in Okayama city in 2017, both of which are located in Okayama prefecture. As per the local board of education in Okayama prefecture, there were 150 reported cases through the app, and they had decided to introduce the app in every state high school in 2018 (Okayama Board of Education, 2018).

Mito (2017) also reported the positive outcome of his program introduced above. He classified students into four groups: (1) "those who want to help and take action," (2) "those who want to help but cannot take any action," (3) "those who don't want to help and so do nothing," and (4) "those who don't want to help but take action" and reported that after implementing the program, the percentages of students in group (1) increased and those in groups (2) and (3) decreased. Furthermore, examining the reason for not helping, he found that after participating in the program, there was a huge decrease of the reason for not helping "due to lack of courage or skills". He concluded that these are the positive outcomes of the program using various apps and materials.

Another app that has been evaluated is the *Jotore*, which was introduced at a private primary school in Gifu prefecture and evaluated by the authors. The evaluation study was conducted at the beginning of the school year using sixth-grade pupils (n = 45) who took classes using the *Jotore* as the experimental group and fifth-grade pupils (n = 57) who had not yet taken classes using the *Jotore* as the control group. In the evaluation study, the participants' awareness of and attitudes toward mobile-phone use and various online risks were examined.

Table 8.1 Mean scores for risk perception, victimization-related anxiety, and beliefs about anonymity (SD in brackets)

	Risk perception (α = .753)	*Victimization-related anxiety (α = .849)*	*Beliefs about anonymity (α = .756)*
5th graders (*n*=57)	2.60 (.67)	2.19 (.90)	1.56 (.63)
6th graders (*n*=45)	2.52 (.70)	2.09 (.73)	1.36 (.57)
Results of t-test	$t_{(100)} = 0.54$, n.s.	$t_{(100)} = 0.61$, n.s.	$t_{(100)} = 1.67$, n.s.

First, we examined their levels of risk perception, victimization-related anxiety, and beliefs about anonymity on the Internet. Kanetsuna (2016) reported that those who had stronger beliefs about online anonymity showed lower levels of both risk perception and victimization-related anxiety, and this led to lower levels of caution about various online risks. Therefore, it was hypothesized that children who learned about online risks with the *Jotore* would show higher levels of risk perception and anxiety regarding online victimization. However, the results were different. There were no significant differences between fifth and sixth graders in any of the above factors (Table 8.1). While the results were unexpected, learning in the *Jotore* class may have changed their perceptions about online risks; with the belief that they could cope, they might have experienced reduced anxiety regarding victimization.

In terms of beliefs about anonymity on the Internet, Table 8.2 below shows the percentages of pupils who responded either "I think so very much" or "I think so" to each question. Overall, most fifth and sixth graders seemed to understand that they are not necessarily anonymous on the Internet. However, there seemed to be more fifth than sixth graders who considered themselves anonymous on the Internet. In particular, about 20% of fifth graders gave a positive response to the statement "It is easy to write something on Internet bulletin boards without being identified." On the contrary, only 10% of sixth graders gave a positive response to this statement. This can be seen as one of the positive outcomes of the practices in the "online morals" section of the *Jotore*.

We then looked at students' perceptions of posting various kinds of information on the Internet. Table 8.3 presents a list covering 12 points of information that can be used to identify individuals and which are often posted on the Internet. The table also shows the percentages of participants who considered it acceptable to post such information on the Internet. It was expected that very few fifth and sixth graders would consider it OK to post them, and the results confirmed our hypothesis. However, among sixth graders, there was not even a single sixth grader who think it OK to post seven out of 12 of the

Table 8.2 Percentages of participants who responded as "I think so very much" and "I think so" for questions regarding beliefs about anonymity on the Internet

	5th graders (%)	*6th graders (%)*	*x^2 test*
You can say whatever you like on the Internet because you'll never be identified.	7.0	6.6	$x^2_{(3)}=0.45$ n.s.
People can talk about anything on the Internet because we don't know each other.	8.8	6.6	$x^2_{(3)}=3.95$ n.s.
You can pretend to be someone else on the Internet.	14.1	11.1	$x^2_{(3)}=1.07$ n.s.
It is easy to write something on Internet bulletin boards without being identified.	22.8	11.1	$x^2_{(3)}=7.15$ n.s.

Table 8.3 Percentages of participants who think "it is OK" to post each information type listed below on the Internet

	5th graders (%)	*6th graders (%)*
My real name	3.5	None
Friends' real names	1.8	None
Teachers' real names	3.5	None
My username/handle name	15.8	20.0
Friends' usernames/handle names	7.0	8.9
Teachers' usernames/handle names	1.8	8.9
My home address	5.3	None
My school name	3.5	2.2
My email address/SNS ID	5.3	None
Pictures/videos of myself	3.5	2.2
Pictures/videos of friends	None	None
Pictures/videos of teachers	1.8	None

information details: those considered "not OK" to post included the person's real name, home address, email address, and pictures and videos. Although there were no statistically significant differences between the fifth and sixth graders, this result could still be considered a positive outcome of the utilization of the *Jotore* in the classroom to teach children about the risks and dangers of posting personal information on the Internet.

Conclusion and future implication

Although many primary pupils and junior high school students possess their own smartphones and use the Internet on a daily basis, their manner of usage is a cause for alarm. Further, some have reported negative online experiences. One of the major root causes of cyberbullying seems to be the common beliefs about anonymity on the Internet. Whether or not they are truly anonymous, such beliefs surely affect users' thoughts and behaviors in various manners. They could induce bullying perpetration and deviant behaviors by giving people a false sense of relief about not being identified or inducing disengagement from personal responsibility and morals. They could also weaken risk perception and the sense of fear regarding victimization, both of which could lead to lowering the preventive attention against various online risks. Therefore, in order to protect children from online risks, it is important to equip them with the necessary information about the possibility of identification on the Internet. Then, various unique characteristics of online communication that are different from face-to-face communication in the real world are should be covered. We must guide children so that they can adequately judge the sites they visit, the authenticity of the information they are receiving, and whether they are causing hurt or discomfort.

As an effective way to achieve such goals, we proposed the use of smartphone apps and online teaching materials. Many children today are already familiar with such apps and materials, and it can, therefore, be easy for schools and teachers to use them in the classroom to teach information literacy and morals. In addition, it is often very useful for children to virtually experience various risk situations in a safe environment as they can learn about the unique characteristics of the Internet and its risks in a realistic manner. Some of the apps and materials introduced in this chapter have already been introduced in schools by some local boards of education, and positive outcomes have been reported. However, the systematic evaluation of the effectiveness of these apps and teaching materials is still insufficient, and more detailed and continuous evaluation must be conducted to determine what types of apps are most effective for which sorts of risk situations. Furthermore, as these apps and teaching materials have only been introduced in some schools, broader implementation is necessary.

Finally, we must remember that apps and teaching materials cannot independently prevent involvement in bullying and deviant behaviors or directly protect children from various online risks. They only give children the opportunity to virtually experience various risk situations and provide them with information about how they should behave on the Internet. The ultimate goal should be to equip children with the skills to adequately monitor and control themselves and take responsibility for their own behaviors on the Internet. We must make the most of these apps to achieve this goal.

References

Aoyama, I., Saxon, T. F., and Fearon, D. D. (2010). Internalizing problems among cyberbullying victims and moderator effects of friendship quality. *Multicultural Education & Technology Journal*, *5*(2), 92–105. doi:10.1108/17504971111142637

Asada, H. and Hara, K. (2017). An empirical study of enlightenment effects in cyberbullying. *Bulletin of the Research Institute of Dokkyo University*, *24*, 55–64.

Bandura, A. (1999). Moral disengagement in the perpetration of inhumanities. *Personality and Social Psychology Review [Special Issue on Evil and Violence]*, *3*, 193–209. doi:10.1207/s15327957pspr0303_3

Bunkeido. (2014). Information utilization training notebook. Retrieved from www.bunkei.co.jp/jotore/

Digital Arts. Lurking danger to smartphone: Virtual experience application. Retrieved from www.daj.jp/cs/sp/app/#csr

Gree. Soul Negotiator. Retrieved from http://corp.gree.net/jp/ja/csr/internet-society/tamaboku/

Hiroshima Kyohan. (2019). Net morals learned in the cases. Retrieved from www.hirokyou.co.jp/netmoral/pdf/pamphlet2019v1.pdf

Ieshima, A. (2019). Ijime x manga: The possibility of prevention education for bullying using manga. *61st Annual Meeting of the Japanese Association of Educational Psychology*, Nihon University, Tokyo, September 2019.

Internet White Paper. (2008). *General Incorporated Foundation of Internet Association Japan*. Tokyo: Impress R & D.

Japanese Cabinet Office. (2019). *Survey on Environment of the Internet Usage for Adolescents*. Tokyo: Cabinet Office, Government of Japan.

Japan Association for Promotion of Educational Technology. (2019). How to walk in the net society. Retrieved from www2.japet.or.jp/net-walk/index.html

Japanese Ministry of Education, Culture, Sports, Science and Technology. (MEXT). (2008a). *The Manual for Dealing with Cyberbullying and Collection of Cases*. Tokyo: MEXT, Government of Japan.

Japanese Ministry of Education, Culture, Sports, Science and Technology. (MEXT) (2008b). *Courses of Study for Primary and Junior-High Schools 2008*. Tokyo: MEXT, Government of Japan.

Japanese Ministry of Education, Culture, Sports, Science and Technology. (MEXT) (2017a). *Courses of Study for Primary and Junior-High Schools 2017*. Tokyo: MEXT, Government of Japan.

Japanese Ministry of Education, Culture, Sports, Science and Technology. (MEXT) (2017b). *Educational Materials for Thinking about New Problems in the Information Society*. Tokyo: MEXT, Government of Japan. Retrieved from www.youtube.com/playlist?list=PLGpGsGZ3lmbAOd2f-4u_Mx-BCn13GywDI

Japanese National Police Agency. (2012). *Public Relations Materials: Status of Crime Information Arrested by the Reports from the Internet Hotline Center in 2012*. Tokyo: NPA.

Kanetsuna, T., Smith, P. K., and Morita, Y. (2006). Coping with bullying at school: Children's recommended strategies and attitudes to school-based interventions in England and Japan. *Aggressive Behavior*, *32*(6), 570–580. doi:10.1002/ab.20156

Kanetsuna, T. (2016). Effects of anonymous beliefs of the Internet on the levels of caution for various online risk behavior. *Paper Presentation at 31st International Congress of Psychology*, Pacifico Yokohama, Kanagawa, Japan, July 2016.

Kashiwa City. (2019). *About the App "STOPit," Which Can Anonymously Discuss and Report Bullying.* Retrieved from www.city.kashiwa.lg.jp/soshiki/271000/p046834.html

Kiesler, S., Siegel, J., and McGuire, T. W. (1984). Social psychological aspects of computer-mediated communication. *American Psychologist*, *39*, 1123–1134. doi:10.1037/0003-066X.39.10.1123

Kyoto Prefectural Police Department. (2019). Experiential net trouble prevention course. Kyoto: KPPD.

Latané, B. (1981). The psychology of social impact. *American Psychologist*, *36*(4), 343–356. doi:10.1037/0003-066X.36.4.343

Mainichi News Paper. (2019). Bullying reporting app effective in Kashiwa of the first introduction to the whole country. *Mainichi News Paper*, July 5, 2019.

Mito, M. (2017). The way of the measures program for the cyber-bullying by the junior or high school student: Through practice to promote the transformation from spectators, a looker-on to an arbitrator. *Study on Development of Teaching*, *10*, 39–47.

Morio, H. and Buchholz, C. (2009). How anonymous are you online? Examining online social behaviors from a cross-cultural perspective. *AI and Society*, *23*(2), 297–307. doi:10.1007/s00146-007-0143-0

NHK. Knock-out bullying Retrieved from www.nhk.or.jp/tokkatsu/ijimezero/

NTT Docomo. (2009). Haruno family mobile-phone story. Retrieved from www.nttdocomo.co.jp/info/news_release/page/090218_00.html

Okayama Prefectural Board of Education. (2018). *Proceedings of the 2nd Regular Meetings of Okayama Prefectural Board of Education*.

Ono, A. and Saito, F. (2008). Educational psychological review about understanding and coping with cyberbullying. *Bulleting of Senri Kinran University*, *5*, 35–47.

Orita, A. (2009). A report on the usernames squatting problem of social-media. *Information Processing Society of Japan Technical Report*, *44*, 5–14.

Pornari, C. D. and Wood, J. (2010). Peer and cyber aggression in secondary school students: The role of moral disengagement, hostile attribution bias, and outcome expectancies. *Aggressive Behavior*, *36*(2), 81–94. doi:10.1002/ab.20336

Saitama Prefectural Board of Education. (2009). Survey results on mobile phone usage: Guidance on prevention and countermeasures for cyberbullying. Retrieved from www.pref.saitama.lg.jp/f2209/ijime/documents/356790.pdf

School Guardian. (2013). Kids' Sign. Retrieved from https://school-guardian.jp/service/kids-sign/

Softbank. Let's think about mobile phone together. Retrieved from https://ace-npo.org/info/kangaeyou/kyouzai/kangaeyou5.html

STOPit Japan. (2018). STOPit. Retrieved from www.stopit.jp/

Sproull, L. and Kiesler, S. (1986). Reducing social context cues: Electronic mail in organizational communication. *Journal of Management Science*, *32*(11), 1942–1512. doi:10.1287/mnsc.32.11.1492

Takeuchi, K., Toda, Y., and Takahashi, T. (2015). How should we cope with smartphone and the Internet problems among adolescence? For further collaboration of society and educational psychologists. *The Annual Report of Educational Psychology in Japan*, *54*, 259–265. doi:10.5926/arepj.54.259

Tokyo Metropolitan Board of Education. Heart Story. Retrieved from http://ijime.metro.tokyo.jp/

9 Commentary

From a Thai perspective

Ruthaychonnee Sittichai and Ram Herkanaidu

Thailand is an East Asian country which has a close historical relationship with Japan. South Korea, Japan and Thailand are all considered to be collectivistic countries as they prioritise the group rather than the individual. Japan though, is seen from our viewpoint as embodying a masculine, competitive society whereas Thailand and South Korea are generally more cooperative and concerned with social harmony. However, it is important to recognise that they all have distinctive cultures and unique traditions/norms which need to be taken into account when designing education initiatives and programmes to counter bullying.

In Chapter 2 it was noted that in Japan, children who have been cyberbullied prefer to talk to friends rather than to teachers or counsellors. In Thailand this is also the behaviour of the majority of victims. This is encapsulated by the Thai concept of *kreng jai*, for which there is no direct translation into English, although its meaning is close to "being reluctant to bother or upset another person". Thus, as a Thai, if I have a problem, I will keep it to myself or perhaps just share it with a close friend, but not with parents or teachers. For this reason, the use of software games and apps may provide a safe space for Thais to gain awareness of the issues and coping strategies relating to cyberbullying and how to access support, an approach which is similar to that noted to be appropriate for Japanese children.

One difference worth highlighting is that South Korea and Japan have specific laws and national policies aimed at tackling cyberbullying, that is, the School Violence Eradication Plan in South Korea and the Bullying Prevention Promotion Act in Japan (see Chapter 2). At the time of writing (2020), there are no similar policies/laws in Thailand. This difference may explain the prevalence of cyberbullying in Thai schools and hence the need for appropriate policies to be introduced. Whereas bullying is represented by the terms *wang-ta* in South Korea and *netto-ijime* in Japan (see Chapter 1), in Thailand, there is no single expression, and how it is described very much depends on the nature of the event. The spectrum goes from relatively harmless *kan yok-lo* (teasing), through *kan klaeng* to *kan rangkae* which is the academic term in Thai for bullying (Mahidol University, 2014).

Increasingly, bullying not only occurs in its traditional forms, commonly thought of as "being physical, verbal, or relational (such as social exclusion), and direct (face-to-face) or indirect (such as rumor-spreading)" (Sittichai and Smith, 2013, p. 32), but also encompasses cyberbullying using mobile phones and the Internet, which is today a common issue. What constitutes repetition of bullying behaviours online is debatable, as even a single online incident can cause lasting harm, while the demeaning content remains accessible online. The nature of power differentials can also be different in comparison to the offline world; for example, the bully might have more advanced information technology skills rather than a bigger, stronger body (Ojanen et al., 2015).

A bullying and cyberbullying study (Sittichai and Smith, 2013) involving 1,049 students aged 12 to 18 years in 12 schools from three provinces in southern Thailand found that 16% of those surveyed had been victims of bullying at least once a month and 14.9% had been victims of cyberbullying. Gender was a significant factor; male students were more likely to be victims, especially cybervictims. In another study of young people in Thailand in 2016, Herkanaidu, Furnell, and Papadaki (2017a) found that among 206 12–18-year-old students, 71% had experienced an interaction online that had upset them. In respect of cyberbullying, 60% said they had been the victim and 44% admitted to being the bully. Further, in as-yet-unpublished data from a similar survey in 2018 involving 352 respondents, the figures for victims and bullies were 55% and 41% respectively. A study jointly conducted by Mahidol University and Plan International Thailand (a development and humanitarian organisation) in 2014 found that 55.7% of respondents who identified as LGBT had been cyberbullied in the past month.

These studies show that traditional bullying and cyberbullying are widespread in Thailand. To find ways to combat this, online safety awareness workshops were carried out in Roi Et and Nong Khai provinces in the north east of Thailand to try out new approaches using active learning strategies (Herkanaidu et al., 2018). The objective of the workshop series was to raise awareness of online safety issues, and in particular, cyberbullying. Such awareness is an indispensable first step to achieving the goal of building digital resilience in young people. The assumption is that young people will have online interactions that are potentially harmful. If they are equipped with strategies and coping mechanisms, they will be better able to manage these interactions.

The theme of the workshops was the principle of gamification that is explored in Chapters 5 and 6. There, a number of games and apps that have proven to be effective in countering bullying are reviewed. One such is the Finnish "KiVa" program, which is well-known worldwide, and uses a combination of interactive multi-media games and group activities, like team-building and discussions. In Chapter 6, the South Korean government-supported app "Angry Daddy" is introduced, which is a game designed for teenagers to learn about cyberbullying and what to do in certain situations. The users work through the game and a chat-like interface, and their responses to certain quiz questions allow them to gain an understanding of important issues. Part of the reason for the development of the game was to find out if educational games, such as “Angry Daddy”, are effective and the research so far shows that they might be.

In the Thai workshops, active learning methods, such as gamification and video-led discussions, were used to explore new ways to engage with young Thais. Most activities were received well by the young people who participated (Herkanaidu et al., 2018), but it was the introduction of a Thai cyberbullying video in the fourth workshop that caused the students to begin to really understand the topic.

The video chosen was an animation as this was thought to be less disturbing and upsetting than a play involving real actors, while still relaying the message relating to the topic. This led to fruitful discussions with students on the nature of cyberbullying, its prevalence and their own coping strategies. They all agreed that it happened a lot but that they rarely told parents or teachers. When asked why not, one student replied that it was not considered to be important to tell their parents. Another replied that they would be blamed if they told someone else. Yet another replied that if someone posted messages with something bad about them, they would retaliate. Similar responses were given in the fifth and final workshop. The use of the video thus opened the door to discussing the issue in a way that made students feel more related to it and to feel less inhibited.

The successful use of the video in the workshops suggests that the utilisation of manga comics and anime (discussed in Chapters 3 and 4) may be good ways of supporting children. Though there are some governmental restrictions, manga is very popular among young Thais. The use of short animations to visualise cyberbullying can help young people to understand and contextualise the problem in their own world. Furthermore, educators can invite children to produce their own artwork/videos on cyberbullying and other online safety materials. The use of visual representations can be a gateway for better discussions and understanding and increased resilience.

Another game-like activity used in the Thai workshops was the Password Challenge (Herkanaidu, Furnell, and Papadaki, 2017b; Herkanaidu et al., 2018), which uses the University of Plymouth’s “rate your password” meter (www.cscan.org/PasswordStrength/). Each student is invited to enter one of their passwords and its strength is then recorded on the board. Weak passwords are those receiving a score of around 40% while very strong passwords would score above 90%. Participants are then given advice about how to create strong passwords and have a chance to improve their score in the second round, when their scores are usually significantly higher. From the experience gained through carrying out these workshops, we were able to confirm that cyberbullying is a major issue faced by Thai youth, yet awareness of the topic is fairly low. Students who were used to a traditional style of teaching responded positively to active learning methods. In particular, gamifying activities and the use of video-led discussions proved effective in raising awareness.

In Chapter 7, the "117 Chat" app is introduced which allows children to report concerns anonymously. That app is similar to "STOPit" (Chapter 5) which allows a person to report acts of bullying or other behaviour, confidentially. On the other hand, "117 Chat" is a 24-hour service that has been developed by the South Korean Metropolitan Police Agency. As well as reporting cyberbullying to their school's police officer, users can also access their counselling service. From our perspective, it would not be difficult to envisage the use of manga, anime, the "KiVa" program and games like "Angry Daddy" in other countries. Reporting apps, on the other hand, like "STOPit" and "117 Chat" require an internal infrastructure to operate within. To bring a service like "117 Chat" to Thailand, for example, would take great effort, inter-agency coordination and investment.

The relationship between anonymity and cyberbullying in Japan is discussed in Chapter 8 and this is a pertinent and open question in Thailand. The nature of Thai society is to be social and communal, and this has crossed over to the digital world. Eighty-two per cent of the population are online and two-thirds of the population are on Facebook (Herkanaidu et al., 2018). The questions brought up in this chapter are rarely discussed or investigated in Thailand, for instance, questions like: "If using a messaging application, do you really know that the corresponding person is actually the person whom you suppose them to be?" Generally you cannot see them and sometimes you cannot pick up visual or verbal clues as to their reaction to your message. In this scenario, miscommunication can easily happen or at least it may be easier to send offending messages. In the figures above for cyberbullying in Thailand, 71% had been upset by an online interaction via messaging.

The chapter ends with a cautionary note, that we should not lose sight of the fact that these educational games, apps, manga, anime and other teaching materials are tools with a purpose. The authors of this commentary chapter agree with this view. The aim should be to promote well-being and instil digital resilience in young people so that they can benefit from the opportunities that being online can offer.

References

Atkinson, S., Furnell, S., and Phippen, A. (2009). Securing the next generation: Enhancing e-safety awareness among young people. *Computer Fraud & Security*, *7*, 13–19. doi:10.1016/S1361-3723(09)70088-0

Herkanaidu, R., Furnell, S. M., and Papadaki, M. (2017a). Online risk awareness and exposure of young people in Thailand. *Presented at the 16th Annual Security Conference 2017, Information Institute Conferences*, Las Vegas, NV, 18–20 April 2017.

Herkanaidu, R., Furnell, S. M., and Papadaki, M. (2017b). Using gamification in effective online safety awareness education. *Presented at the 10th International*

Conference on Educational Research, ICER 2017, Faculty of Education, Khon Kaen University, Thailand, 9–10 September 2017.

Herkanaidu, R., Furnell, S. M., Papadaki, M., and Khuchinda, T. (2018). Designing an anti-cyberbullying programme in Thailand. In N. L. Clarke, S. M. Furnell (eds.), *Proceedings of the Twelfth International Symposium on Human Aspects of Information Security & Assurance. Paper presented at HAISA 2018*, Abertay University, Scotland, 29–31 August 2018. Plymouth, UK: Clarke Furnell.

Mahidol University. (2014). Bullying targeting secondary school students who are or are perceived to be transgender or same-sex attracted: Types, prevalence, impact, motivation and preventive measures in 5 provinces of Thailand. Mahidol University. Plan International Thailand. UNESCO Bangkok Office. Retrieved from https://unesdoc.unesco.org/ark:/48223/pf0000227518

Ojanen, T. T., Boonmongkon, P., Samakkeekarom, R., Samoh, N., Cholratana, M., and Guadamuz, T. E. (2015). Connections between online harassment and offline violence among youth in Central Thailand. *Child Abuse & Neglect*, *44*, 159–169. doi:10.1016/j.chiabu.2015.04.001

Sittichai, R. (2014). Information technology behavior cyberbullying in Thailand: Incidence and predictors of victimization and cyber-victimization. *Asian Social Science*, *10*, 132–139. doi:10.5539/ass.v10n11p132

Sittichai, R. and Smith, P. K. (2013). Bullying and cyberbullying in Thailand: A review. *International Journal of Cyber Society and Education*, *6*(1), 31–44. doi:10.7903/ijcse.1032

10 Commentary from Norway

Natalia Kucirkova

Author's standpoint

I feel privileged to have been approached by the book's editors to write this chapter, especially as I write this text sitting in my office at the University of Stavanger's Learning Environment Centre, which is known for founding one of the most successful anti-bullying programs worldwide. In this commentary chapter, I summarise the broader themes in the eight chapters of the volume and reflect on the lessons learnt and lessons to be learnt in the study of cyberbullying and young children. I begin my account with a short expose of my own professional background and connection to this research theme, followed by some observations on the topics examined by the book's authors. I conclude with some recommendations for future work in the area.

I locate my work at the intersection of psychology, education and human-computer interaction. Given my developmental psychology background, I am mostly interested in the effects of technology on children, acknowledging that these are mediated by the children's parents/caregivers or teachers/educators. In terms of technology, I focus on a phenomenon that cuts across digital and non-digital technologies: personalisation. Personalisation can refer to a practice or process that makes an experience unique to an individual child. For example, a book can be personalised when it was made specifically for one child by her parent or by the child herself. Education as a whole is personalised when it is individualised to individual children in a classroom. Current technologies provide deeply personalised experiences, which can exacerbate negativity (e.g., personalised fake news) but also increase support (e.g., personalised feedback to a student).

My work is grounded in a *literacy as social practice* perspective, building on the inspirational work of Lev Vygotsky, Shirley Heath or Luis Moll, who argued that the purpose and value of literacy are socially and culturally co-constituted. It follows that when it comes to children's use of technologies, the role of culture and community in which children grow up, cannot be separated from the role of technology design and individual children's engagement with it.

In my work I have been able to bring together methodologies that are often isolated from each other, including multimodal analysis with developmental psychology experimental methods. This has allowed me to examine children's interactions with technologies from a rich perspective. It is in the spirit of multi-disciplinarity and multiple methods that I approach the studies in this book and consider their value to teachers, practitioners and policymakers.

Key learning points

There is a consensus among the contributors that the Internet's anonymity exacerbates moral disengagement inherent in bullying and that cyberbullying amplifies the suffering, harm and violence experienced by victims of bullying. The authors consider the interesting question of how much cyberbullying is culturally specific and the possibility of more collective bullying occurring in countries of collective cultural values such as Japan and Korea. The similarities and differences in tackling bullying in South Korea and Japan highlight the role of socio-cultural factors in influencing the origins, perpetuation and eradication of bullying in societies. Another important factor is the specific design of technologies that allow for cyberbullying to spread across time and space. For example, the widely popular messenger application Kakao Talk in Korea has several design flaws that do not support meaningful exchange of information and might further contribute to malicious behaviour. The task of researchers is thus not only to identify which technologies (or which features of technologies) are not helpful, but also which can be used to counteract bullying tendencies. This is evident in chapters focused on producing forward-looking models of media experience, through the use of manga, anime, apps and games, which provide positive immersive experiences. While a lot of extant research has been preoccupied with the negative role of pop culture and modern technologies on children's relationships, the book's authors highlight the anti-bullying role which many popular technologies play in children's lives. I was particularly encouraged by the potential preventive role of games and apps that can support children's resilience and coping strategies. Thus far, however, the potential benefits have been identified mostly on a theoretical level. So that these positive opportunities become an everyday reality for all children, there needs to be a concentrated effort to create an infrastructure of support around vulnerable children. This implies close work with designers who can implement technology features that support healthy social relationships, as well as guidance for teachers and parents on how to use such technologies together with their children. A close collaboration among all adult stakeholders who support children is indispensable and is an issue that needs to be empirically investigated with greater urgency. This brings me to some recommendations for future work in the field.

Key future developments

Most studies reported in this book and in the field are mono-disciplinary, which limits their impact. More multi- and interdisciplinary work is essential to understand the origins, process and outcomes of cyberbullying. Future work in the area should consider collaborative models of knowledge production where effects are not studied linearly (e.g., the impact of an intervention or online program on one outcome) but dynamically, over time, across devices and user groups, with multiple methods. Such work might constitute a paradigm shift for some disciplines while for other researchers it is a natural response to the diverse and democratic society we live in.

Multi-disciplinarity implies strategic collaboration among researchers of various perspectives. One might argue that strategic collaboration is more of a domain of large companies than of educational researchers. Indeed, knowledge concerning effective collaboration strategies is typically reported in management and business journals rather than education or psychology outlets. Simonin's (1997) classic outlines how effective alliances develop iteratively over time, with individuals internalising the collaborative experience. In such an alliance, partners are mutually dependent on each other, as they share goals and strive for mutual benefits (Kale, Singh, and Perlmutter, 2000). Unless we plan and try to work across disciplines, we will not know the benefits. I look forward to future research that is radically interdisciplinary and that not only includes researchers but also designers and teachers as study collaborators.

In the complex and interconnected society we live in, collaboration is no longer optional. The modern world is an interconnected system of people and technologies that jointly co-construct the reality. Technologies such as the Internet of Things literally connect physical and virtual, analogue and digital lives. The key advantage of digital interconnections lies in the efficiency it provides for personalised services and information delivery on scale. The key limitation is the self-governing, fast and often uncontrollable spread of information provided by interconnected systems. Given the high rates of cyberbullying propelled by the Internet contained in stationary computers, the prospect of Internet contained in all technologies seems uncomfortable. The possibility to collect personal data with each service we engage online, and to use these data to personalise the online experience on all platforms that augment our capabilities, including our own bodies, furthers these concerns. Soon enough, it might not be only other people but also other technologies and indeed, our own cyber-persona, that intimidate and frighten us.

I'm not a Luddite, the human thirst for innovations will feed increasing technological progress. The question I am raising for future cyberbullying research concerns the preventative work that needs to happen to nurture fruitful and sustainable anti-bullying environments of trust, transparency and dialogue. Such environments are not created overnight with a one-day professional development course. They are created through everyday conversations online and offline, among teachers, parents, researchers, technology providers and children/young people. Bullying does not happen in isolation. It is a result of compound problems an individual might be experiencing. This is important for schools, teachers and parents to bear in mind and for any programs designed to support anti-bullying strategies.

Some authors in this book imply that a collective culture can exacerbate bullying, which indicates that the solution against bullying lies in collective action. We need to better understand not only the harms but also the significant positives afforded by collective technology use. Researchers need to think more carefully about the concrete implications of their work for the development of anti-bullying technologies (the development of the game "Angry Daddy" discussed in Chapter 6 is a good example of how a simulated role-playing chatting program can affect bystanders' decisions to act as defenders). Technology can serve both positive and negative purposes, as clearly outlined by the Anti-Bullying Network:

> technology is morally neutral and can be a channel for comfort as well as threats. The phone line that carries a threatening text message may also carry information and advice to an anxious parent or a worried child. Whilst technology can be used to bully, the Internet also can be a sanctuary for the victims of bullying by masking their "differences" and allowing them to be part of communities beyond their local one.

Last but not least, we need to ensure that the knowledge about promising technological, theoretical or methodological approaches does not stay in university libraries, but is clearly communicated to parents, teachers and technology designers. I urge anti-bullying researchers to strive for public scholarship that aims to communicate research findings to a wider public beyond the walls of academia through the means of public engagement events, non-academic publications such as blogs, social media posts or magazine articles. Public scholarship is part of researchers' moral obligation of returning knowledge to the community and continuously striving for better versions of ourselves.

Conclusion

It is with the lens of my socio-cultural interest in children's use of technologies that I approached the task of reflecting on the research presented in this book and recommendations for the field. Inevitably, my recent work on the International Collective of Children's Digital Books (Kucirkova, 2017), which brings together researchers, designers and practitioners to develop new literacy apps for children, influenced my recommendation for more collaborative and collective models of anti-cyberbullying research. My goal is to encourage the contributors to this volume, and their readers, to continue the ideas developed in this book through online and offline meetings, in a supportive collegiate environment. This is essential for ensuring that we, as researchers, serve as role models for the relationships we would like to see among the young people we support.

As numerous studies show, bullies follow their victims across many places, from one playground to another one, from Facebook to Instagram or Snapchat to WhatsApp. The codes of conduct on social media and other massive messaging systems need to be agreed collectively, in a serious and transparent dialogue. We all need to act as role models and one supportive community to each other if we are to eradicate cyberbullying.

As researchers we need to make sure that our inquiries are informed by strong theoretical frameworks and strong methodologies. In researching the impact of new technologies, it is easy to be seduced by new forms of data and interests that these technologies bring. Cyberbullying researchers need to strike the difficult balance between remaining true to well-established rigorous methods and theories and be vigilant of new forms of interaction afforded by new technologies. Last but not least, researchers need to act as role models for other researchers in the field. In the Learning Environment Centre at the University of Stavanger, we take this message to heart. We eat lunches around one big table in a shared office area, we care for and about each other beyond the professional arena, we celebrate joint successes of publication or grants with genuine pride for the other and have fun at social events such as bowling, kayaking or hiking in the mountains. Such small acts of kindness are not trivial; they are the steps in the step change that is necessary for preventing and dealing with bullying wherever and whenever it occurs.

References

Antibullying Network, Information on Reacting to Bullying. Retrieved from www.antibullying.net

Kale, P., Singh, H., and Perlmutter, H. (2000). Learning and protection of proprietary assets in strategic alliances: Building relational capital. *Strategic Management Journal*, *21*(3), 217–237. doi:10.1002/(SICI)1097-0266(200003)21:3<217::AID-SMJ95>3.0.CO;2-Y

Kucirkova, N. (2017). iRPD: A framework for guiding design-based research for iPad apps. *British Journal of Educational Technology*, *48*(2), 598–610. doi:10.1111/bjet.12389

Simonin, B. L. (1997). The importance of collaborative know-how: An empirical test of the learning organization. *Academy of Management Journal*, *40*(5), 1150–1174. doi:10.2307/256930

11 Commentary

From a North American perspective

Samuel Y. Kim and Stephanie S. Fredrick

The timing of this book could not be more serendipitous. With researchers struggling to find a strong, efficacious method of combating bullying (e.g., Merrell et al., 2008; Yeager et al., 2015), the current text emphasizes the need for understanding both the effect of culture and the coming and growth (Kowalski, Limber, and McCord, 2019) of cyberbullying. In particular, the editors have set the context of both bullying and cyberbullying within the framework of the Korean and Japanese cultures. Though these countries are proximal to one another, there are notable differences in how bullying is perceived. For example, the exploration of *Wang-ta* and *Ijime* (the Korean and Japanese terms for "bullying") within each country and how it has been addressed and changed over the years brings to light important differences including common types of cyberbullying, such as Kakao Talk Prisons and LINE Hazushi. Kakao Talk Prisons, as described in Chapter 1, is a type of cyberbullying where a group of people will continually force a person into a chat room within a popular chatting app and regularly barrage the person with negative comments. Whereas LINE Hazushi actively excludes a person from a chat group by making new groups without the person in a popular chatting app in Japan. With factors such as exchange of cultural practices and immigration, it would not be surprising to see these methods of cyberbullying begin to permeate the psyche of other cultures.

Though the prospect of the new insidious types of cyberbullying can be disheartening, there is quite a summary of multiple and innovative attempts to address this problem. For example, in Chapter 3, the discussion of the LIME model provides a type of cyber-ecological model to help understand cyberbullying. This framework is a novel expansion of the social ecological model into the cyber world, and it provides a way for future researchers, educators, and parents to consider how children interact with the cyber world. For example, the authors of Chapter 8 explore how the LIME model is used to educate and categorize a cyberbullying experience. Additionally, it can provide a way to systematically address cyberbullying issues and potentially pave the way for combatting some moral disengagement techniques such as dehumanization (Bandura, 2016).

There seem to be attempts to address bullying and cyberbullying by taking advantage of cultural interests and technology. For example, Chapter 4 discusses the use of manga and anime as a method of combating bullying and cyberbullying. The authors suggest that bullying prevention and intervention can be augmented through the use of this medium of sharing stories and entertainment. Though this could be dismissed as being culturally specific to Japan, the authors take considerable care to point out the popularity of manga and anime in other countries, potentially affecting those children in those countries. With technology, a few of the chapters discuss the apps that are designed to intervene and prevent bullying. Some of these apps were designed with support from the government, demonstrating how an established institution can intervene and prevent bullying in creative and novel ways. As the pace of change within the world of cyberbullying is ever changing, it is encouraging to see innovations in ways to intervene, such as apps designed to report cyberbullying to apps that immerse users in a cyberbullying experience.

In light of these strengths within the text, it is important to emphasize the call for more cross-cultural research in cyberbullying. Research that examines measurement invariance is necessary in examining the construct of bullying across cultures and using psychometrically sound measures of cyberbullying. As noted in Chapter 1, certain aspects of bullying and cyberbullying may be less prevalent or relevant in certain cultures (e.g., social exclusion) and perhaps should not be compared directly. These differences may be further enhanced by different modalities for cyberbullying (e.g., LINE, Kakao Talk). Given the use of the Internet and related tools are very common among Japanese and Korean cultures, it is reasonable to assume that these tools may have differential effects cross-culturally. This has important implications for the creation and implementation of culturally sensitive bullying prevention and intervention methods.

Anonymous reporting apps are commonly used by schools and companies across the globe and although some government agencies report their effectiveness in terms of number of incidents reported (see Chapter 8), more rigorous evaluation studies are needed to determine the efficacy of these apps—as well as learning apps that teach Internet safety—as it relates to bullying prevention. Further, questions remain regarding who is most likely to use these apps (e.g., youth, parents, schools) and under what conditions anonymous reporting or learning apps are most effective. As wisely stated in Chapter 8, our ultimate goal is for youth to independently engage in appropriate and respectful behavior online and apps may be one tool of many that we can utilize in this endeavor. In the United States, schools are increasingly focusing on teaching students social and emotional learning skills—such as self-awareness, relationship skills, and problem solving—both offline and online (i.e., digital citizenship skills; Gleason and von Gillern, 2018) in order to reduce problematic behavior, strengthen relationships, and boost academic achievement (Durlak et al., 2011). Given the focus of bullying and cyberbullying within a social ecological framework (Cross et al., 2015; Swearer and Hymel, 2015, see also Chapter 2 of this text), future research is needed in terms of which systems these apps are most appropriate or most effective (e.g., individual, parent, teacher, school, community).

Further, research is needed regarding the generalizability of the use of technology for cyberbullying prevention across cultures. For example, manga and anime have increased in popularity in Western cultures, but using popular visual media for bullying and cyberbullying prevention, or as an educational tool—as referenced in Chapter 4—in North America has not been explored. Instead, North America has focused on reducing cyberbullying through popular social media apps (e.g., Instagram, Facebook, Twitter, YouTube, TikTok) by creating reporting or blocking systems or allowing users to delete comments or make accounts and video private. Instagram recently created a feature that allows users to restrict comments, which makes the comment invisible to all users except the individual who posted it. However, these features focus on intervening after the incident has already occurred; thus, much work and collaboration is needed to investigate how to use popular visual media or learning apps to prevent cyberbullying from occurring.

The editors of this book, along with the authors, have presented in a single volume the advancements of cyberbullying in two Asian cultures. What is unique is the presentation of both the advancements of the methods of cyberbullying as well as the interventions and prevention efforts. Readers of this volume will gain cultural insight and consider how cultural specificity is critical to understanding this phenomenon. Additionally, international readers are likely to gain inspiration of innovative methods of understanding cyberbullying and intervention methods being used in other countries. Though these strengths are clear in the text, there is also a clear need for further scholarly work in this area. Several apps and methods that were described are truly innovative, but rigorous empirical study is only emerging at this time. It is hoped that among the audience of readers, there are researchers ready to answer the call and address the lack of rigorous study of the methods and cultural generalizability. By answering the call, perhaps the field can eventually be one step ahead of cyberbullying instead of following in its wake of constant and nefarious change.

References

Bandura, A. (2016). *Moral Disengagement: How People Do Harm and Live with Themselves*. New York: Worth Publishers.

Cross, D., Barnes, A., Papageorgiou, A., Hadwen, K., Hearn, L., and Lester, L. (2015). A social-ecological framework for understanding and reducing cyberbullying behaviours. *Aggression and Violent Behavior*, *23*, 109–117. doi:10.1016/j.avb.2015.05.016

Durlak, J. A., Weissberg, R. P., Dymnicki, A. B., Taylor, R. D., and Schellinger, K. B. (2011). The impact of enhancing students' social and emotional learning:

A meta-analysis of school-based universal interventions. *Child Development*, *82*, 405–432. doi:10.1111/j.14678624.2010.01564.x

Gleason, B. and von Gillern, S. (2018). Digital citizenship with social media: Participatory practices and learning in secondary education. *Educational Technology & Society*, *21*, 200–212.

Kowalski, R. M., Limber, S. P., and McCord, A. (2019). A developmental approach to cyberbullying: Prevalence and protective factors. *Aggression and Violent Behavior*, *45*, 20–32. doi: 10.1016/j.avb.2018.02.009

Merrell, K. M., Gueldner, B. A., Ross, S. W., and Isava, D. M. (2008). How effective are school bullying intervention programs? A meta-analysis of intervention research. *School Psychology Quarterly*, 23, 26–42. doi:10.1037/1045-38-30.23.1.26

Swearer, S. and Hymel, S. (2015). Understanding the psychology of bullying: Moving toward a social-ecological diathesis-stress model. *American Psychologist*, *70*, 344–353. doi: 10.1037/a0038929

Yeager, D. S., Fong, C. J., Lee, H. Y., and Espelage, D. L. (2015). Declines in efficacy of anti-bullying programs among older adolescents: Theory and a three-level meta-analysis. *Journal of Applied Developmental Psychology*, 1–16. doi:10.1016/j.appdev.2014.11.005

Index

Note: Page numbers in italic indicate figures and in bold indicate tables on the corresponding pages.

For Product Safety Concerns and Information please contact our EU
representative GPSR@taylorandfrancis.com
Taylor & Francis Verlag GmbH, Kaufingerstraße 24, 80331 München, Germany

www.ingramcontent.com/pod-product-compliance
Ingram Content Group UK Ltd.
Pitfield, Milton Keynes, MK11 3LW, UK
UKHW021507240926
475702UK00035B/651

* 9 7 8 0 3 6 7 2 0 2 4 2 2 *